READING
FABLIAUX

GARLAND REFERENCE LIBRARY
OF THE HUMANITIES
(VOL. 1805)

READING
FABLIAUX

Norris J. Lacy

GARLAND PUBLISHING, Inc.
New York & London / 1993

Library of Congress Cataloging-in-Publication Data

Lacy, Norris J.
    Reading fabliaux / Norris J. Lacy.
        p.   cm.—(Garland reference library of the humani-
ties ; vol. 1805)
    Includes bibliographical references and index.
    ISBN 0–8153–1510–4 (alk. paper)
    1. Fabliaux—History and criticism. 2. Narrative poetry,
French—History and criticism. 3. Humorous poetry,
French—History and criticism. 4. French poetry—To
1500—History and criticism. 5. Tales, Medieval—History
and criticism. 6. Literary form. I. Title. II. Series.
PQ207.L33   1993
841'.0309—dc20   93–8245
                                            CIP

Printed on acid-free, 250-year-life paper
Manufactured in the United States of America

For Richard O'Gorman

CONTENTS

Preface

Preface

This little volume is unusual in several ways. By design, it is not a typical academic book in either conception or execution. It is comparatively brief, it does not proceed from a particular thesis that is to be argued, and although it deals with the fabliaux, it does not begin to discuss all the texts that ostensibly belong to the genre. My project, as my title indicates, is far more modest: to read fabliaux and offer some observations drawn from those readings.

That purpose itself marks this as an unusual book, at least compared with other studies of fabliaux. This is not intended as an extravagant claim, and in fact I have no desire to justify my book by measuring it against the real or imagined deficiencies of others. On the contrary, I am pleased to acknowledge my debt to scholars and critics whose efforts have helped to rescue the fabliaux from the literary dustbin to which they were once largely relegated, dismissed as bourgeois, naive, or indecent.

Yet, despite the value and, in some cases, the excellence of recent studies, they have not succeeded in solving a fundamental problem inherent in studying a genre composed of some 150 texts. Specifically, scholars have most often responded to the need to say something applicable to the entire genre, something concerning fabliau publics, for example, or fabliau parody, or women in the fabliaux. The results, unfortunately, tend to lose sight of the individual fabliau in a forest of generalizations about *the* fabliaux. That is, that approach makes it virtually impossible to discuss all the crucial elements of a text, and it is no less difficult to discriminate between the numerous fabliaux that are crafted with care and subtlety and those, equally numerous, that are crude compositions of little or no literary value.

Charles Muscatine's book on the fabliaux illustrates just how difficult it is, within the confines of the traditional approach, to do justice to the individual text. I hasten to note that in singling out his study I do not intend any condemnation: indeed, all things considered, his may well be the best recent book on the fabliaux. Precisely for that reason, it provides the best illustration of the method mentioned above. For example, to demonstrate the "disparity between female needs and desires on the one hand, and female speech on the other," Muscatine (p. 123) notes that the husband in *Le Sohait desvé* (titled *Le Sohait des vez* in Noomen) falls asleep, leaving his wife sexually aroused. She declines to disturb him, because it would be unseemly for a woman to do so. When she does fall asleep, she has an erotic dream and accidentally awakens her husband. Muscatine's reference to these events effectively illustrates his point but, on the other hand, omits the most memorable aspect of the fabliau: the fact that the dream concerned a marketplace where every booth sold penises of all sizes and descriptions. The point Muscatine is making does not require that information and would in fact be blunted by its inclusion. But it is nonetheless true that his approach, which is that of most fabliau scholars, does not allow for a presentation of the full narrative, and that in turn complicates the problem of defining fabliau art and conveying a proper sense of the appeal of these texts.

Conversely, the articles that scholars have devoted to the analysis of a particular fabliau or limited group of texts may well reveal a good deal about the comic art of one or more authors, but they rarely place the text in its generic or cultural context.

A desideratum at this point is therefore a study that manages to combine the close *reading* of particular texts with a synthetic treatment of the genre. I believe some of the practical problems posed by the number and variety of fabliaux can be solved by moving from analysis to synthesis, rather than the usual, opposite method.

My method, like that of other fabliau scholars, has been to organize a chapter around a specific, major preoccupation of fabliau authors or of their modern critics. However, instead of beginning with a discussion of the problem and illustrating it with a variety of examples, I begin each chapter with a close reading of a single, carefully chosen fabliau; from there, either I move to the general subject (as in the chapter on genre) or, more often, I first expand the focus of my comments to other related texts and, only then, to general conclusions about the problem under consideration. Such a method will not enable me to avoid generalities, but I hope at least to arrive at them only after a detailed analysis of particular works. Thus, while I discuss a number of the traditional concerns of fabliau criticism, my focus also remains firmly on the techniques of fabliau authors and on the literary value of the works themselves.

In my first chapter, I examine a fabliau text in considerable detail, to demonstrate both the literary sophistication and some of the literary problems of the best fabliaux. Thereafter, my readings are by no means exhaustive analyses or formal *explications de textes*, but several of them, especially in the initial chapters, are reasonably extensive commentaries, and I can only hope that the detailed analyses do not prove tedious. Most of the readings are less detailed and are meant simply to point out a few of the characteristics of a specific work that illuminate the problem dealt with in the chapter.

Readers may find my method unsettling, not only because it is unconventional to begin by a systematic reading of a specific text, but especially because that analysis leads me inevitably to make frequent observations not necessarily related to the announced subject of the chapter. That approach continues in the more general discussions following the analysis of the primary text. In the chapter on "courtliness," for example, I do indeed discuss the courtliness of the text in question and of other texts, as well as the use of courtliness for parody, but I also continue the discussion of taxonomic questions from my second chapter, and I deal with other, quite different, matters, such as the relationship of surprise to fabliau humor.

Thus, in a sense, the focus of a chapter is provided by a particular text rather than by a single problem or theme, and, as I suggested, the central problem of a chapter (e.g., generic identification) may well be treated, at least briefly, in several sections. In fact, a preoccupation with the humor of the fabliaux is evident in every chapter and, implicitly, on practically every page.

Similarly, a specific fabliau may be mentioned or discussed more than once. Rather than try to mention all or most fabliaux in the course of the volume, I provide links from chapter to chapter by exploiting a kind of "sub-corpus" of texts that merit discussion, effectively elucidate themes and methods, and are in some degree representative compositions. Most of the fabliaux that I analyze in detail, and a few that I discuss only briefly, reappear in three or four chapters. Consequently, although I make mention of well over fifty texts, I offer detailed readings of only ten, briefer commentaries on perhaps twenty, and passing remarks about the others.

One runs a risk, as I suggested, in adopting an untraditional organization or approach, but I trust that the reader will find something to commend my choice. In fact, I hope to contribute modestly both to an appreciation of the compositional technique and style of some of the most accomplished fabliau authors, and to an appreciation of the richness and the variety of the fabliau genre, all too often "homogenized" by critics whose work, however admirable, is prevented by the conventional approach and organization of fabliau studies from conveying their sense of that variety.

Given those goals, this volume clearly has a premise, if not a thesis. It is that the fabliaux deserve to be studied as autonomous works of art that are far more than items of evidence about a genre in general or, especially, about a particular class or historical period. Consequently, my project—simply to read fabliaux, to observe their materials and methods and evaluate the effect of those methods—will be justified if I am able to demonstrate the diversity of these texts and the remarkable craftsmanship of many fabliau authors, as well as the narrative ineptitude of some.

My study departs from most preceding ones in at least one additional way, made possible by the progress of Noomen's important edition: I often draw citations or conclusions from manuscripts other than the one used for the base text. Dangers attend such an approach; although the very existence of variant manuscripts affirms the autonomy of each (as a natural and inevitable phenomenon and as the form in which a text was known to a segment of the medieval audience), it does not follow that all manuscripts and readings are equal. Medieval scribes do make mistakes; medieval redactors may ruin a good story while trying to improve it. Nonetheless, access to all manuscripts of a fabliau will alert us to other readings and other interpretations. Thus, in some chapters I discuss the ways our understanding of a fabliau would be transformed if we simply read a different manuscript. The result is to multiply texts, and while that proliferation sometimes presents us a bewildering collection of variants, it undeniably corresponds more closely to the medieval literary experience than does reliance on a single critical text, however competently prepared.

Finally, the style and tone of my study may also diverge from the traditional. This book is by design informal, straightforward, and, I hope, unpretentious. First, I am intentionally writing for the student and generalist no less than for the professional medievalist. My style furthermore reflects not only my audience, but the subject as well, and my own tastes. In previous essays, I have found an impersonal academic style to be a less than entirely congenial vehicle for dealing with the humor, not to mention the frankness and sexuality, of the fabliaux, and I have felt most comfortable with a more informal style. Humor is necessarily personal, and accordingly I see no justification for writing impersonal and formal prose about texts characterized by the quest for entertainment, humor, and good fun.

I have made other concessions to the fun and narrative interest of the fabliaux: I have referred more often and more directly to the stories themselves—the ruses, puns, seductions and failed seduction attempts, reversals, and complications—than I would be tempted to do in treating most other subjects. After rereading and teaching fabliaux repeatedly over some twenty-five years, I still enjoy them no less, and frequently much more, than on first reading. By occasionally recounting a full episode when a detail would suffice to make my point, I hope to share some of that enjoyment with readers.

*

My introductory section offers a sample reading of one of the better fabliaux and then discusses some of the assumptions about fabliaux and the problems inherent in their study. The next two chapters—and I call them "chapters" for convenience, even though their brevity hardly justifies the term—are also prefatory in a sense. The first of them offers a reexamination of the definition of fabliaux. My contention is that usual definitions of the genre artificially restrict our understanding by imposing rigid generic boundaries, thereby excluding from consideration works that may be very much like fabliaux—or that may in fact *be* fabliaux. This is hardly revolutionary genre theory, and much of what I say in that chapter has been said before, on more than one occasion. However, considerations that may have become commonplace for other genres have not always penetrated fabliau criticism; I am therefore persuaded that my views in this section, while admittedly lacking originality and theoretical sophistication, have significant practical application.

The following chapter (III) is a brief treatment of one aspect of the genre's ethos: I suggest that behind the illicit relationships, cruel deceptions, and outrageous jokes there lurks a fundamentally conservative spirit that endorses what is simple, natural, and direct and that urges the maintenance of the status quo in relationships between classes and sexes.

Chapter IV investigates one of the traditional assumptions of fabliau scholarship: fabliau misogyny, a phenomenon that cannot be denied but that deserves to be defined with more precision than has been done in the past. My original plan called for this chapter to be paired with a study of anticlericalism in the fabliaux, but a rereading of texts persuaded me that there was comparatively little to be said on the latter subject: the fabliaux are very often "anti-priest" but not really anticlerical—or, if they are, this view is sufficiently generalized to provide little material for analysis and only minor interest for readers.

To make a transition from matters of genre and theme to method, I offer a chapter on the problem of courtly language and parody in the fabliaux. This question, which some might consider to have been settled by Nykrog's pioneering work in 1957, has been reopened in recent years, notably by Ménard. In discussing courtliness, I also refer back (as I do in other parts of the book as well) to the matter of generic definition: why and how is a "courtly fabliau" considered a fabliau?

The following two sections (VI and VII) bring us, I believe, to the heart of the book: studies of the uses and power of language in the fabliaux and of the narrator's voice and role. Next, VIII deals with a few of the numerous methods and processes exploited by fabliau authors to produce humor, often by shaping reader expectations and playing on them for comic purposes.

The final chapter before my conclusion examines closure, the ways fabliaux end. In the process, it necessarily discusses the morals appended to many texts; those morals—some fitting, some not—are a frequent closural device, and there are a number of problems attending the means authors used to bring a fabliau to a close.

*

A couple of disclaimers are in order, in regard to the vocabulary and approach of my study. I occasionally refer to the "reader," for that is the way we now must generally experience fabliaux. That is, of course, historically inaccurate, for the fabliaux were obviously made for oral presentation, and they would clearly be most effective if we could hear them in a skilled oral performance. It is apparent that the psychological processes involved in hearing a story or a joke are quite unlike those of reading. Nonetheless, I have retained the term for convenience and sometimes use it interchangeably with "audience"; it is intended to refer both to the modern reader and the medieval listener.

Somewhat more hesitantly, I have not always insisted strictly on the distinction between author and narrator or, especially, between either of them and the "implied narrator." Theoretically, the distinction is essential, but it is of minimal practical importance throughout much of my discussion. I do respect that distinction wherever the failure to do so would distort an interpretation or mislead my reader. For example, in the chapter on narrative voice, I make the point that the author specifically *creates* a personalized and even dramatized narrator, endowing him with a voice with which he can comment, sometimes inaccurately, on his themes and characters. In those cases, I am careful to speak of the narrator and not confuse him with his maker.

Finally, even if I accord myself the comparative luxury of examining ten fabliaux in some detail, I admit to having neglected certain classes or kinds of fabliaux. As I note in my conclusion, I have expended less effort on the explication of moralizing tales than on erotic stories and on the accounts of various kinds of ruses. That choice reflects my own preference for humor over moralizing, but one might also justify it by noting that many traditional studies of the fabliaux, perhaps because of moralistic scruples or embarrassment, tended to avoid the more frankly scabrous texts.

I have appended to my study an alphabetical table of all fabliaux I have mentioned. There I indicate the edition used and the volume number and inclusive pages for each text. That permits me, within the text, to refer to fabliaux only by title and, when specific passages are cited, line number. An exception is made for the fabliau discussed in some detail at the beginning of each section, where I give the same information as in the alphabetical listing. I use the following sigla to indicate editions: *N* (Noomen and van den Boogaard, which I have used for all the fabliaux included in the six volumes that have appeared to date); *MR* (Montaiglon et Raynaud, for most of the others), *L* (Livingston, for the edition of Gautier le Leu's fabliaux), *ED* (Eichmann and DuVal). For fabliaux not included in Noomen's corpus (or planned for that edition but not yet published), I have most often chosen to use Montaiglon-Raynaud, despite the serious deficiencies of that collection, rather than superior editions scattered here and there. For most purposes, the accessibility of *MR* partially compensates for their editorial deficiency; wherever necessary, however, I correct or complement their texts by recourse to manuscripts or to another edition. Full publication information on editions will be found in the bibliography. In referring to fabliau texts, I generally use the title exactly as given in the edition used, but I have occasionally taken the liberty of regularizing the use of diacriticals to conform to current editorial practice with Old French texts.

The early work on this volume was supported by a generous grant from the American Council of Learned Societies; I am grateful for that support and am happy to acknowledge it.

I also wish to thank the editors of three journals for permission to incorporate into this volume some material previously published in their pages: *L'Esprit Créateur* for "The Fabliaux and Comic Logic," 16.1 (1976), 39-45; *Romance Notes* for "Fabliau Women" (in a special number entitled *The Ideology of Courtly Romance*, ed. J. Burns and R. Krueger), 25.3 (1985), 318-27; and *Reading Medieval Studies* for "Fabliaux and the Question of Genre," 13 (1987), 25-34.

Above all, I am grateful to Richard O'Gorman. Some thirty years ago, at Indiana University, he first introduced me to the study of fabliaux, and he later directed my dissertation. Ever since, he has supported and encouraged my work on fabliaux, as well as on medieval romance and other subjects, and he read portions of the manuscript of this book and offered very helpful comments reflecting his admirable and customary command of textual matters and of related scholarship. To recognize his guidance, his support, and especially his friendship, I am happy to dedicate this volume to him.

St. Louis, March 1993   N.J.L.

I. Introduction

Text: *Cele qui se fist foutre sur la fosse de son mari*

124 lines
Noomen, III, 377-403

*[At a man's burial his widow throws herself weeping upon his grave
and resists all attempts to console her or to make her leave. Before
long, a knight and his squire approach, and the latter wagers that he
can seduce her despite her grief. As the knight watches from a distance,
the squire greets the widow, but in response to his "May God save
you," she informs him that her only wish is to die. He reveals that he
is ten times as unhappy as she, because he had given his love to a
beautiful and courtly lady whom he had later killed. The widow asks
how he caused this death, and he replies that he did so by means of
sexual intercourse, whereupon the grieving widow expresses the desire to
perish the same way. He willingly does her bidding, but the act brings
her pleasure rather than death, and her grief is forgotten.]*

This fabliau, the title of which refers to a woman "who got
screwed on her husband's grave," is a recasting of a portion of the
Matron of Ephesus story known from Petronius and found in well
over a dozen medieval French texts.[1] It provides intriguing material
for an introduction to the fabliau form, for behind the façade of a
dirty joke we will discover a surprisingly subtle and sophisticated

---

[1] The French texts include a fable, *De vidua*, by Marie de France, apologues in two
other *Ysopet* collections, and a narrative inserted in Matheolus's *Lamentations*. For a
full discussion of the theme, see my *La Femme au tombeau: Anonymous Fabliau of the
Thirteenth Century* (diss., Indiana University, 1967). In that dissertation I also provide
a detailed examination of this fabliau, and I have reworked material from those pages
for the present commentary. Further observations on this text are offered in my
article "Types of Esthetic Distance in the Fabliaux," in *The Humor of the Fabliaux: A
Collection of Critical Essays*, ed. Thomas D. Cooke and Benjamin L. Honeycutt
(Columbia: University of Missouri Press, 1974), pp. 107-17.

narrative, depending for its effect not only on physical humor and comedy of situation, but also on the expert manipulation of irony and courtly parody. This text is clearly one of the masterpieces of the genre, and it moreover belongs to the group identified by Per Nykrog as *fabliaux classiques*, the thirty or so fabliaux whose survival in three or more manuscripts attests to their popularity during the Middle Ages.[2] We can thus be reasonably confident that, if we consider this text to be an outstanding comic creation, our views and those of medieval audiences coincide.

However, as we shall eventually see, the fact that *Cele qui se fist foutre sur la fosse de son mari* is something of a minor masterpiece may make it less than an ideal representative of the genre. The same could probably be said of masterpieces of most if not all genres and periods: although we may be tempted to use them to define a genre, they inevitably define themselves, as it were, transcending the limits of the form to which they belong. A detailed commentary on this fabliau will both demonstrate its excellence and, ultimately, dramatize a number of the problems that attend any generalizations about fabliaux.

The fabliau's introduction is a standard and very brief overture to the anecdote. It is of interest for its use of the word *fable*, which in this instance, as in a good many others, can mean only fiction or lie[3]; this author intends, he says, to tell us not a "fable," that is, not a fiction, but a fabliau that is true. This may well be nothing more than the equivalent of the assurance, given by a teller of jokes, that "this really happened." On the other hand, we should recall that truth, for the Middle Ages, was not necessarily what was empirically

---

[2] Per Nykrog, *Les Fabliaux* (Copenhagen: Munksgaard, 1957), pp. 324-25. In addition to *Cele qui se fist foutre*, the list of *fabliaux classiques* includes a number of fabliaux we would doubtless expect (*Auberee, La Borgoise d'Orliens, Aristote, Le Bouchier d'Abeville, De la dame escoillee*, perhaps even *Le Pet au vilain*), but also some whose apparent popularity may surprise us. The latter category is most dramatically represented by *La Couille noire*, a decidedly unengaging text for modern tastes.

[3] In other instances, as taxonomic designations, "fable" and "fabliau" appear to be interchangeable terms (see the following chapter). Line 62 of this text offers yet another meaning: there the knight accuses the squire of fabricating "si grant fable" (referring to the latter's intent to seduce the grieving widow). Noomen's glossary (s.v. "fable") refers to this line and defines the word as "idée fantaisiste," an incredible or outrageous notion.

verifiable: the author may be telling us not that the event actually occurred, but that it is "true" because it possesses exemplary value or is firmly anchored in documentary or oral tradition.

In his haste to proceed to the tale itself, the author spends very little time setting the stage. His brevity continues even after the narrative itself is begun. Beyond the simple fact that the husband died "en Flandres jadis" ("in Flanders, formerly," 7), the author makes reference neither to geography nor to time. The personages are themselves given no names. They are in fact types or stock characters: the rich man and his wife, the knight and his squire. Of the wife, who is the central figure in the fabliau, we learn nothing beyond the fact that she was "de sa mort irie" ("distraught over his death," 9), and, for initial purposes, that suffices. Furthermore, the use of a stock character brings to the widow's role a degree of universality and lends increased weight to the author's generalizations concerning women: he observes—and his fabliau is devised to demonstrate it—that they are by nature fickle and faithless (13).

Given the anonymity of the characters and the generality of the descriptions, we may be surprised by the narrator's reporting of two small details. One is the fact that the husband had formerly been poor but had then become wealthy ("Uns hom, qui de mout po d'avoir / Ert en grant richece enbatuz," 4-5). The other is the information, offered during the widow's lamentations (28), that she was pregnant. Both may well be presented simply to emphasize the dimensions of her loss and provide additional reasons for grief. The information about her pregnancy, followed by her question, "Qui gardera l'anfant et moi?" ("Who will care for my child and me?" 29), is a particularly plaintive lament—although subsequent events may alter our reading of this line.

Depictions of the woman's grief occupy almost one-fourth of the entire text and divide distinctly into three parts, in addition to the initial statement (8-9) that she "Molt fu . . . de sa mort irie." The division into three sections is signaled by the use of *Qant* or *Et quant* ("when") to introduce each one and to suggest the passage of time, from the husband's death through the preparations for the burial ("Et qant ce vint a l'anterrer," 21) to the completion of the interment itself.[4] Most important, the progression from one section to the next adds incrementally to our understanding of her grief.

The first section uses third-person narration to present the visible and audible evidence of her grief:

> Qant la dame vit devié
> Son seignor, qui l'ot tant amee,
> Sovant s'est chaitive clamee;
> De grant duel demener se poine.
> Mout i enploie bien sa poine:
> Ses poinz detort et ront ses dras,
> Et si se pasme a chascun pas.

("When the woman saw her beloved husband dead, she proclaimed her misery; she took pains to express her grief. She made great efforts to do so: she wrung her hands and tore her clothing, and she swooned repeatedly," 14-20)

In the second section, the narrator continues to describe her grief, and then he constructs a monologue to present the widow's words in direct discourse. That passage is clearly the peak of her grief, its most frenzied and immediate expression:

> Et qant ce vint a l'anterrer,
> Lors oïssiez fame crier
> Et dementer et grant duel faire,
> Que nus ne lo porroit retraire.
> Et aprés s'escrie sor toz:
> "Biaus sire chiers, o alez vos?
> Or vos met l'an en cele fosse!
> Sire, je remain de vos grosse!
> Qui gardera l'anfant et moi?
> Mon voil morissiens nos endoi!"

---

[4] This attempt to depict the passage of time is somewhat unusual in the fabliaux, whose authors are more likely simply to *tell* us that time passed. This fabliau is not unique in its use of such a technique, however, and a similar effect is created in *Le Vilain de Bailluel*. There the wife succeeds in persuading her stupid husband that he is dying; more precisely, she informs him that he will die, then (a few lines later) that he *is* dying, finally that he is dead.

("And when it came time to bury him, then you would have heard the woman cry and grieve and lament so bitterly that no one could describe it. And then she cried loudly, 'Dear good husband, where are you going? Now they are placing you in this grave! Sir, I am pregnant with your child! Who will care for it and for me? I would prefer that we both die!' " 21-30)

The third division leaves off the direct discourse but (in a passage excluded from Noomen's critical edition[5]) continues to emphasize, for several more lines, the violence of her lamentations; the accumulation of present and simple past tenses portrays her actions directly and without qualification. Then, beginning with line 31, the narrator makes a sudden change of direction and method. He shifts the focus away from her to those around her, and, more important, he also begins to multiply imperfect and conditional tenses. The result is the dissipation of the intensity and immediacy that had been previously generated. Only in line 37 is there a perfect tense that returns us to the immediacy of the action, but the subordination in verses 36-37 ("Fort [*Tant* in MS. *A*] se conbat et fort estrive, / *Que* il l'ont laissiee par anui"), by emphasizing less her actions than their effect, further removes her from the narrative focus and prepares for the arrival of the knight and squire.

---

[5] Here I am referring to lines preserved in MSS. *A* and *E*, but not represented in Noomen's critical text. They follow line 30 in his text, and I thus designate them 30a-d. My justification is that *A* is clearly the superior manuscript and should have been the base manuscript for a critical edition. Noomen's base text is instead *B*, and his reasoning is curious. He points out (III, 377) that *A* is "exécutée avec soin. La graphie et la versification sont correctes . . . . A plusieurs endroits, il se distingue par la qualité de ses leçons." And yet, simply because it shares the merits of *A* (the best manuscript) and of *C* (for which he offers qualified praise), he has chosen *B*, a manuscript that he criticizes for "un certain nombre de lapsus et de négligences" and for the addition of a more extended epilogue "d'allure peu soignée" (III, 378). My use of lines 31a-d (with my punctuation) thus does not represent a desire simply to complete the pleasing symmetry of the three stages of the woman's grief; it also—and especially—reflects my preference for the most reliable text, which should certainly have served as the base manuscript. However, there is an additional justification for the use of other manuscripts, should such justification be required; see my comments (especially n. 9 below; also in the preface and passim) concerning the value of variant redactions.

[Quant li cors fu en terre mis,
Dont s'escria a mout hauz cris,
Si se deschire et pleure et brait;
A la terre cheoir se lait.]
Si parent la reconfortoient;
A l'ostel mener la cuidoient,
Mais ele dit ja n'i iroit,
Ne ja ne s'en departiroit
De la fosse, morte ne vive.
Fort se conbat et fort estrive,
Que il l'ont laissiee par anui.

("When the body was placed in the earth, making her wail with loud cries, she tore at herself and wept and wailed; she let herself fall to the ground. Her relatives comforted her and wanted to take her home, but she refused to go and said that she would never leave the grave, dead or alive. She struggled and fought until they eventually gave up and left her there," 30a-d, 31-37)

Thus, the depiction of her grief dramatizes its successive stages, from an impersonal description to a dramatic presentation of the woman's own words to another descriptive passage reporting her words and actions and her relatives' departure. Apparently, the townspeople have been impressed by the depth of the widow's sorrow, and they have also given up efforts to console her. In fact, however, the indirection of the last few lines has clearly blunted the force of her emotion, and the attentive reader will surely be watching here for confirmation of the narrator's earlier prediction: a woman's grief is soon forgotten.

At this point, the author turns from preparation to intrigue, that is, to the seduction itself. As the knight and squire approach the cemetery, the former expresses the noble sentiment we might anticipate from him: "g'en ai mout grant pitié" ("I feel great compassion for her," 50). In sharp contrast to his style and sensibility are the scheming mind and the unadorned language of the squire, who not only considers the knight's idealistic reaction to be misplaced, but also understands the character of women far better than does the nobleman. Neither sentimental nor naive, he shocks the knight by wagering that he can seduce her. Typically, though, he is far more blunt than my summary indicates: he does not in fact say, "I'll seduce her," but rather "La foutrai" ("I'll fuck her," 57).

However, once he begins to speak with the widow, his language contrasts strikingly with his crudely confident prediction. In fact, his initial words to the woman constitute an unmistakable pastiche of the courtly style. It is language we would expect instead from the knight, and to an extent the humor of the work grows precisely out of the squire's assumption of courtly language and manners. The encounter with the widow is amusing and comical, not simply because the squire attempts to seduce her and succeeds, but rather because his artifice in this attempt involves behavior that is incongruent with his character and intent and that properly belongs to the courtly code. Thus, he addresses her by the conventional courtly "Chiere suer" ("dear lady," 72), and when she expresses the desire to die, he uses courtly clichés to explain how he killed his own lady-love:

> "Je avoie tot mis mon cuer
> En une fame, que j'amoie
> Plus mout assez que ne devoie,
> Que mout estoit cortoise et sage:
> Ocisse l'ai par mon ostrage"

("I gave my heart entirely to a lady, whom I loved inordinately and who was very courtly and wise; I killed her through my excess," 82-86)

When she asks him just how he had done that, he combines two registers—low and high, or the common and the courtly—in a single, wonderfully comical line: "En fotant, doce amie chiere" ("By fucking, my fair dear lady," 88).[6]

We may well have found his uses of the word *foutre*, juxtaposed to courtly formulas, startling as well as humorous, but the widow is evidently less easily shocked than we. Instead, without hesitation, she

---

[6] Busby makes a related point about *La Grue*; this composition begins "as a serious courtly poem," but when the young woman asks the young man whether she can purchase the crane he has caught, he agrees to sell it for "un foutre." See Keith Busby, "Courtly Literature and the Fabliaux: Some Instances of Parody," *Zeitschrift für romanische Philologie*, 102.1-2 (1986), 72.

invites the same treatment, and the squire does not have to be asked twice: he immediately complies with her request. Thus, making prominent use of the formulas of the courtly code, he easily seduces the lady within view of the knight who had just expressed his profound compassion for her. The scene thereby makes a mockery of such compassion, and the discrepancy between the reality of the situation and the knight's compassion constitutes an implicit but compelling condemnation either of courtliness itself or of the knight's particular brand of courtly illusions.

At this point, however, our attention must return to a line already mentioned: "Et tost a grant duel oblié" (13), that is, "she [woman] has quickly forgotten her great sorrow." But this statement concerning feminine inconstancy, while expressed unequivocally and illustrated vividly in the fabliau, remains ambiguous, because it does not specify *when and how* a woman forgets grief. In this fabliau, is the forgetfulness the cause or the result of the seduction? In other words, is the narrator simply announcing in advance the outcome of the story, that is, telling us that the squire, by his blandishments, will be able to *make* the widow forget her grief? Or is he indicating that, in what he takes to be typically female behavior, she will inevitably and promptly forget that grief of her own accord and thus become easy game for a seducer?

Our interpretation of the entire fabliau turns on our understanding of this line. If her grief is genuine and undiminished when the squire and knight find her, then the fabliau is simply the story of a cynical squire cruelly tricking a poor grieving, and astonishingly naive, widow. Hearing that she wants to die, he hints that she could be killed by sexual intercourse; gullible to the end, she invites such a death, and in the moral appended to the text the author is able to make a telling point about the faithlessness of women. (One wonders, though, whether the moral of the story should not logically concern the stupidity of the woman rather than her faithlessness.)

If we reread the fabliau with care, however, we find an alternative and, to my mind, more persuasive explanation: that is the notion that gradually, if not indeed from the very beginning, the widow begins to feign grief for the sake of appearance.[7] The first of many keys to such a reading is the narrator's insistence on the visible and audible evidence of her grief (e.g., "Lors oïssiez fame crier," 22), rather than on her actual emotion. The widow's *relatives and friends* are thus the ones who are impressed by her constancy, whereas the author offers us knowledge denied to the characters themselves: while the latter see only the protestations and manifestations of grief, we are decidedly privileged observers, who understand the true nature and limited extent of that grief. This double vision—this contrast between appearance and reality—is the source of the impressive irony of this fabliau.

The text offers ample support for this interpretation. For example, we are told not that she was grieved, but that her grief was expressed in a particular way: she was greatly saddened *par sanblant et par dis* (8), and even if her initial sorrow were genuine, the author assures us such sorrow will not last (13). The contrast of appearance and reality is maintained in the descriptions of her grief up to and during the burial. We see the continued shift of attention from a fact to the circumstances accompanying it. Thus, she carefully sets about mourning ("De grant duel demener *se poine*," 17, emphasis added here and in the following quotations), and it is clear that she goes through these motions consciously ("Mout i enploie bien sa poine," she "makes efforts," 18), and manuscripts *A* and *E* underline her competence in such affairs: "Qu'ele en a le molle trové," ("for she knew well how to do it," MSS. *AE*, 19). Her actions convinced at least the townspeople: "Ce *samble* a toz vers son seignor / Ainz fame ne fist tel dolor" (MS. *A*, 21-22). Evidence of her sorrow could be *seen* and *heard* (24-32). Finally, as she falls upon the grave, the author remarks that "A la terre cheoir *se lait*" ("she lets herself fall," MS. *A*, 36).

To be sure, any of these formulas, taken alone, could be an entirely neutral statement. Even the last ("A la terre cheoir se lait") does not irrevocably establish her duplicity; the expression *se laissier*

---

[7] Although the alternative explanation I offer strikes me as far more sensible and defensible, I nonetheless believe that the pretense of naiveté is a crucial element of the humor, and we should not simply dismiss it without a second thought. For further reflections on the possibility of dual motivations in this and other fabliaux, see my concluding chapter.

+ verb is a common enough locution in medieval texts and does not automatically imply calculation.[8] But the multiplication of such formulas, as well as the narrator's insistence that her lamentations convinced *others*, can leave little doubt, long before the squire's arrival, of her insincerity.[9] Seen from this angle, the fabliau is far more complex and subtle than a casual reading would suggest. The squire understands that the widow's grief, whether initially sincere or feigned, has surely been forgotten, simply because that is in the nature of woman. She, however, has backed herself into a corner by refusing to leave the grave until she is released by death; the squire simply offers her a way out of that corner, a way to save face and justify her actions by inviting death, while in fact getting on with her life.

Having followed the text to this point, we may also wonder again about the woman's lament concerning her pregnancy (28). Since she had not mentioned her condition at the beginning, we must now inquire about her protestations: does she emphasize her predicament to increase sympathy? The answer to that is doubtless affirmative, but to a related and provocative question—whether the pregnancy may itself be a fiction—we cannot give a legitimate answer.

---

[8] However, see again *Le Vilain de Bailluel*: the woman undresses her "dead" husband, puts him to bed, closes his eyes and mouth, and "Puis se lest cheoir sor le cors" ("lets herself fall on the body," 59). In fact, except for the crucial fact that the husband in *Cele qui se fist foutre* really is dead, the two scenes resemble each other—in the line from *Le Vilain de Bailluel* just quoted, in the woman's manifest lack of sincerity, and in her lament: "Frere, dist ele, tu es mors: / Dieus ait merci de la teue ame! / Que fera ta lasse de fame, / Qui por toi s'ocirra de duel?" ("Sir, she said, you are dead: may God have mercy on your soul! What will happen to your distraught wife, who will kill herself with grief over you?" 60-63).

[9] This fabliau is an excellent, if very subtle, test case for Jean Rychner's thesis (in *Contribution à l'étude des fabliaux: variantes, remaniements, dégradations* [Neuchâtel, 1960]), according to which variant versions of particular fabliaux may have been prepared with different intentions or with different publics in mind. As my analysis shows, a portion of the evidence for the widow's insincerity exists in only two of the manuscripts (*E* and the best manuscript, *A*; see above, n. 5). Only two conclusions are possible: either the evidence I have adduced *should* have been in Noomen's edition or we must acknowledge two redactions, the distance between them slight but not without significance. In the latter instance, one redaction emphasizes the initial faithlessness of the widow more strongly than does the other, although her ultimate perfidy is of course never in doubt in either group of manuscripts.

Speculation is tempting but ultimately unwarranted by textual implications.

In any event, while seducing the woman, the squire clearly does not victimize her. Instead, we can only conclude that he merely presents to her an opportunity that she welcomes. If she was indeed feigning grief, at least by the time the squire arrives—and I do not think another reading is easily defensible, even in Noomen's edition—and if she has announced her intention to remain there until she dies, she has created for herself a dilemma that can be resolved only by the agency of someone else.

And in their encounter, each of the protagonists has met his or her equal in deceit. She has taken care to maintain the appearance of grief and to conceal her real emotion; and the squire, disguising *his* own nature behind a courtly façade, permits her to take her pleasure and rationalize it as well. It is amusing that this lady, with her own haughty pretenses, commits the act with a squire, but he is in a sense her male counterpart. The appearance-reality contrast is here applicable to both of them: both *pose* as something they are not, and as a result they succeed in satisfying the same *real, physical* desire.

The knight's role presents another textual and interpretive difficulty. The contrast between the two male characters, ostensibly providing an obvious if implicit critique of courtly ideals, appears to be the principal justification for his presence in the fabliau: he has no direct part in the action, but he functions as the backdrop against which the excesses of his code are dramatized. The difficulty here, however, is that it is less than entirely clear how he reacts to the seduction. Lines 100-01 in the Noomen edition tell us that the squire seduces the widow "Si que ses sires bien lo vit: / De rire se pasme a bien poi!" ("In the sight of his master: / he nearly died laughing"). Given the punctuation, as well as the choice of base manuscript, it is clear that Noomen reads the "he" of line 101 as a reference to the squire, enjoying his success and the discomfiture of the knight.

However, had Noomen selected for his base text the superior manuscript, *A* (see n. 5), or, in fact, *any* manuscript *except* the one he chose, the lines in question would have read "Si que ses sires bien le vit / Qui se pasmoit de ris en aise" ("so that his lord saw it [him?], who fell down laughing"). Even these lines are problematic, though, for as the bracketed translation suggests, they contain a syntactic ambiguity. There are several possible readings. If the pronoun *le* refers to the act rather than the actor, then the knight is clearly laughing; if *le* is the squire, then either the knight or the squire could be laughing (the antecedent of *qui* could be *ses sires* or *le*). The last of these possibilities strikes me as unlikely, however, and unless we insist on seeing the knight as a shocked and perhaps outraged observer, we will be more likely to take *ses sires* as the antecedent, in which case it is "his master . . . who nearly died laughing." The difference is crucial, for in the latter case the fabliau illustrates not only the cynicism of the squire, but also the inauthenticity of the knight's espousal of courtly values.[10] The squire then serves as the agent for the unmasking of the widow *and* the knight.

This problem illustrates graphically how our reading is affected by the editor's choices. Not only does *A* contain more persuasive evidence of the widow's insincerity, but the knight, in *A*, also appears to enjoy the seduction almost as much as the squire does. I am not arguing that this *fabliau* necessarily provides a critique of the knight, but only that *one manuscript or one redaction* of it clearly does so.

However we may read the knight's reaction, the humorous action of the fabliau is supported as well by comedy of character and comedy of dialogue. While the nature of comedy is not the primary subject of this essay, my analysis of the composition suggests that the humor is consistently based on an incongruity introduced into the text. The seduction itself is, as I have said, in sharp contrast to the outcome that a widow's bitter laments would ordinarily lead us to expect. Furthermore, the fabliau utilizes for its effect the discrepancies between the manners of the knight and squire, between the normal speech of the squire and the tone of his words to the lady, between this courtly tone and the sudden return to his accustomed style ("En fotant"), and finally between a logical response to this

---

[10] Benjamin L. Honeycutt reads the fabliau as I do (although it must be noted that the MR text, the one available to him in 1974, is edited so as to encourage that reading). Honeycutt, referring to the knight's "vulgarity," calls him a "voyeur knight" and insists that he is "feigning shock at his squire's proposal" (91). Speaking of the typical fabliau knight, he points out the extent to which that character's conduct is "at comic variance with his role in epic and romance" (76). See "The Knight and His World as Instruments of Humor in the Fabliaux," in *The Humor of the Fabliaux: A Collection of Critical Essays*, ed. Thomas D. Cooke and Benjamin L. Honeycutt (Columbia: University of Missouri Press, 1974), pp. 75-92.

statement and the desire she immediately expresses to meet a similar fate by identical means. Thus, the author's success in the composition of this fabliau is due to his repeatedly directing our focus squarely on an aspect of the story and then brusquely resolving this attention in a manner that is unexpected—but that, if we have read with sufficient care, is nevertheless entirely justified and in character.

The fabliau's irony, more heavily coloring the redaction represented by MS. *A*, extends through the entire work, beginning with our knowledge (10-13) that the woman's grief would shortly be assuaged. Our awareness that she will not meet the fate that she pretends to long for precludes the arousal of the pity and sympathy that would inevitably inhibit humor. Then, with the exposition of the squire's intent, we know even what will happen, and our interest is transferred from the outcome of the fabliau to the manner of its accomplishment.

The joke has been told, and told effectively, and in this poet we have a storyteller who knows when to stop. Thus, he hastily concludes with an observation concerning the inconstancy of woman. This moral is not unsupported by the anecdote preceding it, as in a good many fabliaux, and the deviousness of woman is a common medieval theme, but in this case it appears to be a convenient closural device: the reader senses that the pleasure to be derived from telling and hearing a good story is the central point of this text. And, to be sure, the narrator's skillful and economical narrative technique and his masterly handling of irony and humor have produced an exceedingly well-told tale, which must be considered a masterpiece of the fabliau art.

*

In addition to offering us an excellent comic narrative, which rewards reading and commentary, this fabliau provides a useful point of departure, both because it shares many of its concerns and features with other texts to be discussed in subsequent chapters and especially because it is a near-perfect embodiment of many traditional assumptions about fabliaux in general.

- A brief, humorous narrative, it fits perfectly the classic definition of the fabliaux: Bédier's formula, "un conte à rire en vers."[11]

- This text also accomplishes its comic purpose with the exemplary economy that is an acknowledged characteristic of the fabliaux. Its author eschews excessive detail and distracting commentary alike, carefully crafting virtually every line to contribute to the desired effect.[12]

- Its intrigue, like that of the majority of fabliaux, is erotic in nature.[13]

- It deals with the cupidity and deceitfulness of women; moreover, like a great many fabliaux, it condemns women both implicitly and, in the moral, explicitly.

- Fabliaux tend to accentuate the ruses and deceptions by which an object is obtained, an act of revenge committed, or a seduction accomplished. At least ostensibly, this text does the same, although we have seen that the widow is neither naive nor necessarily victimized.

- This fabliau also makes very specific, and in this case cynical, use of courtly language and images. Despite popular assumptions about the bourgeois context of the fabliaux, use of (or play on) courtly formulas is characteristic of a good many fabliaux.

- I will on several occasions deal with the indeterminacy of certain textual elements, such as the question of the knight's reaction to the seduction.

---

[11] That is, "a comic tale in verse"; see Joseph Bédier, *Les Fabliaux: études de littérature populaire et d'histoire littéraire du moyen âge* (Paris, 1894; 6th ed., Paris: Champion, 1964), p. 30.

[12] In contrast to *Cele qui se fist foutre sur la fosse de son mari*, most of the other medieval settings of the Matron of Ephesus tale multiply complications, such as the theft of a body from the cemetery and, in some instances, the mutilation of the husband's cadaver. The fabliau eliminates all conceivable distractions in order to concentrate on the central, crucial intrigue.

[13] That is, it is erotic in a technical sense: it concerns sexual intercourse. Of course, it is far from being "erotic literature" in another sense, that of exciting prurient interest in the reader. The latter is foreign to the purpose of fabliaux.

• Finally, the discussion of this text permitted us to draw conclusions from manuscripts or redactions not represented in the critical text, and that variance (or *mouvance*) of texts is a crucial feature of fabliau art that will be a recurrent emphasis in the pages to come.

In short, were we to seek the text that best exemplifies the characteristics of, and traditional assumptions about, fabliaux—what they are about, what they are like, how they work, how the narrator exercises his craft—we might justly select *Cele qui se fist foutre sur la fosse de son mari*. And, in addition, I have suggested that, in terms of its narrative excellence and its comic value, this text must also be counted among the dozen or so best representatives of the fabliau genre.

But therein, as I further suggested, lies a difficulty: the best representative of any literary form is never a truly representative example. There exist excellent and pointless jokes, admirable and execrable romances (and novels, poems, dramas), and sublime and ridiculous fabliaux, and the masterpieces of any form inevitably constitute their own categories, in contradistinction to ordinary or inept texts. But the fabliaux offer special problems not encountered when we deal with modern genres and even certain other medieval forms.

As we shall see, it is by no means a simple matter even to *define* a fabliau, and Bédier's famous formula has little beyond its pithiness to commend it. Furthermore, contrary to certain received ideas, reflected in my remarks above, it is not true that most fabliaux, or even all the best of them, narrate their story with the "exemplary economy" or the comedic success we have observed in *Cele qui se fist foutre*. And, whereas we might justifiably praise the unity of this text, which has neither digressions nor distractions, we will encounter some other fabliaux that merit praise, although—or because—they multiply intrigues, narrative details, and even digressions and distractions. Even in terms of morals or of the treatment of women, the genre is far less predictable than we might expect; while many fabliaux vilify women, either for lascivious conduct or for deception (or both), we will also encounter women who are admired or praised for their skill in deception or who indulge their sexual appetites with impunity.

Thus, my analysis of this text will not tell us just what a fabliau is, or what it is like, but no other choice of texts would have been better for that purpose. At best, it will illustrate only one *kind* of fabliau, but from the outset I expected to do no more than that. In fact, my intention throughout this volume is precisely to refute any notion of the uniformity of the fabliaux. Were it indeed possible to describe a "typical" fabliau, this book would be unnecessary and seriously misguided.

To appreciate fully the radical dissimilarity of many fabliaux, we have only to contrast *Cele qui se fist foutre sur la fosse de son mari* to other fabliaux, beginning, rather dramatically, with *Du prestre et du mouton*, by Haisel. The latter text, which at eighteen lines is the shortest extant fabliau, involves a priest making love to a married woman. A sheep sees the priest's head moving and butts it; the fornication ceases; the moral is, "it's wise to be prudent"; and so ends this fabliau. Stretching a point, one might at best praise the narrative economy of the anecdote; otherwise, there is little here either to praise or even to discuss, beyond noting, perhaps, that the moral curiously counsels prudence while appearing unconcerned with condemning illicit sex. Subtlety, ruse, linguistic playfulness, genuine humor, and all the other elements that make *Cele qui se fist foutre* a success are simply lacking in this text.

La Crote, at sixty-two lines, is also short and uncomplicated.[14] A husband asks his wife if she can guess what he is holding in his hand. She guesses incorrectly that it is his penis; in fact, it is his testicle. The woman then wagers with her husband that, even with three guesses, he will be unable to identify the substance she has in her hand. He feels and smells it and twice guesses incorrectly; only when he finally tastes it does he triumphantly identify it correctly as excrement.

This text may not be quite as pointless as it seems, and I discuss it briefly in the chapter on fabliau women. For the present, it stands merely as an example of a particular kind of fabliau, involving the simplest of jokes told with impressive crudeness. In terms, again, of narrative sophistication, command of irony, mastery of subtle

---

[14] The introductory lines of this text emphasize the value of brevity in fabliau composition; ". . . li fablel cort et petit / Anuient mains que le trop lonc" ("short and brief fabliaux are less boring than those that are too long," 4-5).

detail, and manipulation of courtly registers, *Cele que se fist foutre* is entirely unlike this work. Both are short and both are meant to be humorous; beyond that, it would not be easy to identify them as representatives of the same genre.

But at least they *are* humorous. Some fabliaux are not and were not necessarily meant to be. To complete this picture of the fabliaux, we would have to add at least two other examples, one, like *Le Preudome qui rescolt son compere de noier*, that differs from the texts discussed above by its moralizing intent and that therefore, for some critics, may not be a fabliau at all,[15] another, like *Estormi*,[16] in which narratorial commentary is so disruptive as to blunt the humor of the situation, perhaps a third to represent longer fabliaux, in which methodology is necessarily modified to a considerable extent. Even then, we would have a very incomplete introduction to the fabliaux, thus proving my point: in terms of their length, complexity, character, method, and effect, no introduction can effectively convey the diversity and interest of fabliaux, any more than we could expect a brief introduction to the novel (for example) to provide a paradigm that will comfortably accommodate all novels.

The ideal approach to this problem—to read all the texts that belong to the genre and those that, if not fabliaux, are at least related to them—is beyond the limits of this volume. However, I hope the following chapters will make a useful start; they will "read" a few fabliaux in some detail, beginning with a text, *La Veuve*, that is distantly related to *Cele qui se fist foutre sur la fosse de son mari*.

---

[15] Concerning the exclusion of moralizing or other texts from the fabliau corpus, see the next chapter.

[16] For an analysis of *Estormi*, see Chapter VII.

II. Questions of Genre

Text: *La Veuve*

By Gautier le Leu
502 lines
MR, II, 197-214

[A woman whose husband has died appears to be inconsolable. She weeps, wails, and protests that she will never be comforted. Soon, however, she begins to be tormented by sexual appetites. The remainder of the story depicts her interior monologues, her conversations with others, and the process by which she procures a replacement for her husband. She taxes this man's sexual prowess, exhausts him, and then reviles him, comparing him unfavorably with her former husband. The two of them quarrel and he beats her; however, after a suitable delay, they reconcile at least temporarily.]

To begin this chapter, I have chosen to discuss a text that scholars have sometimes taken, though incorrectly, as an analogue of *Cele qui se fist foutre sur la fosse de son mari* (see Chapter I). Both texts present widows who initially grieve for their husbands but soon forget them. The general situations, and perhaps the attitudes toward women, are thus strikingly similar, but narratively they have little or nothing in common. *La Veuve* contains comparatively little action. It consists of conversations and of interior monologues; Muscatine praises it for offering some of the best dramatic monologue to be found before Chaucer.[1] The work offers as uncompromising a condemnation of woman as we are likely to find in the fabliaux corpus: she is fickle, shrewish, hypocritical, and ruled by an insatiable desire for sex.

---

[1] Charles Muscatine, *The Old French Fabliaux* (New Haven: Yale University Press, 1986), p. 70.

Gautier's narrator begins by addressing "Sangnour" ("Lords"), evidence that the fabliau is addressed specifically to men, not to people in general. He emphasizes the fact that every man will eventually die or, as he puts it (2-3), be called to an army from which no one returns; and he then turns his attention to the widow left behind. The early portion of the tale presents the narrator's view of a typical widow's typical reactions: she must be restrained, she cries out about her pain and grief, and she expresses her desire to die (10-22).

Readers of fabliaux will not be surprised to learn that her grief will not endure. The narrator, in fact, is hardly subtle: he informs us that at the entrance to the church the woman again begins her *mestier* (her "task" or work) of weeping and wailing (23-25), and Livingston's edition goes even farther, telling us directly that there was no truth in her words ("Ensi va acontant ses fables / Qui ne sont mie veritables," L 23-24).[2] The funeral service offers us generalizations about the clergy as well: the priest is eager to proceed to the offering (27) and thus hastens the service.

When the husband is buried, Gautier tells us that anyone watching her tremble and pound her fists together would think her likely to lose her mind (36-40). Shifting the focus from reality to appearances, that is, from what she does to the reactions of those watching her is a technique (used more systematically, as I noted in chapter I, in *Cele qui se fist foutre sur la fosse de son mari*) that casts additional doubt on her sincerity.

The following lines (41-42) offer details that signal a new dimension to the story. Ostensibly, this scene, in which the woman's lamentations resume at the door of her home, largely duplicates the events that occurred in front of the church, but this time there is a difference: her grief is no longer a general response that might be representative of bereaved widows. It is instead a quite specific allusion to this couple's recently improved economic condition and

---

[2] The MR edition is based on an obviously defective manuscript, and my comments about the conclusion refer to Livingston's more reliable edition. The line numbers, too, both in this reference and in a number of later ones, are from Livingston and are indicated by the "L" preceding the numbers. See Charles H. Livingston, *Le Jongleur Gautier Le Leu: étude sur les fabliaux* (Cambridge: Harvard University Press, 1951).

even to his sartorial condition: his clothes fit him very well, especially
the new suit made for him at New Year's (56-62).

These passages are the first example of the widow's and the
author's pervasive concern with money and possessions. We might
have expected the narrator to suggest that faithless women are more
concerned with material possessions than with emotional ties, but
reference to recent economic changes and to clothing are details of
a union that cannot be representative of all marriages and that thus
individualizes this woman. Consequently, while her general reactions
are presented as characteristic of *women*, these details are particular
to *this woman*. The author has in these few lines created a complex
figure, embodying in the woman both the generality that makes her
the representative of her sex and the specificity that makes her into
a particular literary character with a sharply defined personality. That
specificity is what transforms this text from an abstract misogynistic
diatribe into an anecdote that we can with some justification consider
a fabliau. Or, more accurately, it is both an abstract diatribe and an
anecdote, but the abstractions are forgotten for the moment, and they
will resurface only much later, when narrative design requires them.

The specificity continues as the widow gives details of two recent
dreams that predicted the man's death. She then talks about another
dream she had, in which her husband broke a hole in the wall of the
house, after which a beautiful dove came to her and made the wall
whole (67-84). She protests that she does not understand the meaning
of that dream. We, on the other hand, do, for whereas Gautier's
technique may be subtle, his thematic development is not—and surely
was not meant to be. He has left no doubt that her grief will be
assuaged and that she will find a replacement for her husband.

That process does not take long, although it is recounted in several
stages. First, the woman objects when she is told that she should find
another man (89-104), but soon she conceives an intense hunger for
char crue (raw meat)—not for peacock or crane, but rather for the
"dangling sausage" desired by so many (123-26); as a result, she is no
longer concerned with death (127). She then begins to evaluate as a
potential partner every man she meets (60-68), and she begins to
ignore her children, blaming them for her inability to attract a man,
and finally she starts to mistreat them (194-206). There follow both
monologues and conversations with her neighbors. Finally, we are
told, she captures her prey (388).

Here, for the first time since the early lines, the narrator reverts to generalizations, this time about men. He uses the singular *man*, but the universality of the observation is clear: once caught, a man can consider himself lost (389ff.). Thus, as is often the case in fabliaux, observations that are literally about men actually refer obliquely to women: regardless of the man's sexual skills, he is despised the next morning, and the woman insults him and compares him unfavorably to her late husband. The impression of generality is soon countered, however, by additional specific details, concerning thirty marks that, according to the lover, the woman had promised him (423-26). They quarrel, he beats her, and once she has mended, they are together again (449-76), because as long as a man can perform his sexual duties well, his faults (e.g., beating the woman!) can be overlooked (477-78).

Gautier concludes with a curious moral, which is addressed to "You who despise women . . ." (L 563), but instead of the anticipated condemnation of women, he offers an unexpectedly tolerant opinion: that the pleasures of sex make it worth a man's while to defer to a woman (L 564-70). He notes, for example, that when his own wife is troublesome, it is better for him to leave than to hit her with a piece of wood (L 577-78). Submissive men, he concludes surprisingly, have more pleasure than aggressive ones (L 582-83). Livingston, like others before him, concluded that the moral was a later addition to the text (p. 163). Yet, even though there is undeniably a disjunction between the subject matter and the moral, the latter is hardly a spirited defense of women; it is instead a further confirmation of certain traditional (that is to say, negative) attitudes toward women and some advice, perhaps ironic, designed to help men make the best of a bad situation.

Not only the summary of the text at the head of this chapter, but the analysis as well omits many of the fascinating details, such as those concerning the "catalogue of worldly goods advertising the widow's wealth" (Muscatine, p. 62). The portrait of the woman, and much of the appeal of the story in general, depend on the accumulation of details that define the texture of this work. Similarly, those details enable Gautier to translate what begins as generalizations about women into a striking and very specific presentation of an individual, who, as I noted, nonetheless remains a representative of her sex. There can be few characters in medieval texts of this brevity who reveal themselves so thoroughly and effectively to us. That revelation is lost in summary.

But what must interest us in particular is the question of how, if at all, we will categorize this work. Muscatine indicates (p. 54) that it has "hardly any plot at all," and that is obviously correct if we contrast *La Veuve* to a fabliau like *La Borgoise d'Orliens*. Yet, there is at least an elementary plot, produced precisely by the progressive individuation of the widow and by her search for a man to replace her husband; the curious status of that plot appears to situate *La Veuve* on the fringes of the fabliau genre, if it belongs to it at all, and thus serves to illuminate some of the problems attending the discussion of fabliaux and, in a larger sense, the question of any medieval literary "genre." Is the work a fabliau?[3] And is the answer to that question determined by plot, by "spirit" (see following paragraph), or by some other criterion?

La Veuve is listed as a fabliau by Bédier and Nykrog but is excluded from the corpus by Noomen and van den Boogaard. Schenck calls it a "non-typical fabliau" and a tale "to be reclassified," owing to its absence of conflict and its long description of the widow; she defines it rather as a *tableau de moeurs*,[4] a term first applied to it by Bédier (p. 480). Hellman and O'Gorman, too, cite Bédier's term *tableau de moeurs*, noting that *La Veuve* is not "a story in the strict sense of the word"; they contend nonetheless that it is "a fabliau in spirit."[5] Finally, Muscatine, while assigning this text to a group of compositions that have "hardly any plot at all," nevertheless refers to it as a fabliau (p. 54). So do I, but less because it neatly fits a specific definition of "fabliau" than because, as I will suggest, it is unproductive, if not simply impossible, to craft a definition so precise as to include or exclude "peripheral" texts; thus, the term "fabliau," though

---

[3] In fact, Gautier's text, in Livingston's edition, refers to itself as a romance (L 592).

[4] Mary Jane Stearns Schenck, *The Fabliaux: Tales of Wit and Deception* (Amsterdam: John Benjamins, 1987), pp. 68-69.

[5] Robert Hellman and Richard O'Gorman, trans., *Fabliaux: Ribald Tales from the Old French* (New York: Crowell, 1965), p. 157.

imprecise, is surely as good as any other in instances where generic terminology is essential.

*

Generic questions are of capital importance for the medievalist, not least because our own notion of "genre" is a postmedieval invention—a fact that should make us look with some skepticism upon the generic pronouncements made either by medieval authors or by critics. Zumthor, among others, expresses considerable distrust of the very term "genre," although at times he follows tradition and uses it for the sake of convenience.[6] It is true that any generic grouping inevitably entails some degree of distortion, as it emphasizes similarities among texts while blunting differences. To circumvent that difficulty we might in theory try to reject all groupings of works and simply speak of texts—individually. The advantage of such an approach, however, would be short-lived, since writers, readers, and critics, who obviously need to categorize and compare works, would surely replace one set of labels by another.[7]

Whenever we deal with a text that does not coincide with our understanding of a particular genre, we inevitably react in one of two ways: we either exclude the text from the genre or we broaden the boundaries of the genre. The latter phenomenon, especially, is quite common for modern literature, from the eighteenth century to the present. Works like *Tristram Shandy, Finnegans Wake, A la recherche du temps perdu* or representatives of the *nouveau roman* all required us to rearrange the limits of the genre. But if we are more or less accustomed to the progressive extension of generic borders in modern literature, we seem to resist it for the Middle Ages. Despite frequent critical assertions to the contrary, we continue in practice to conceive of *chansons de geste, romans,* and fabliaux as discrete generic entities, and where they appear to overlap or merge (as with a text like *Huon de Bordeaux,* an epic that often seems less epic than

---

[6] *Essai de poétique médiévale* (Paris: Seuil, 1972), p. 160.

[7] For that reason, I will continue to use the term "fabliau" and to discuss texts commonly identified as such. That does not alter the fact that the uncritical acceptance of traditional terminology is indefensible.

romance[8]), we are likely to leave our generic conceptions intact and consider the particular work an anomaly.

Problems of taxonomy constitute a particular affliction in fabliau studies, both because of the contradictory generic pronouncements made in the texts themselves and also because of the tyranny of Bédier's definition ("contes à rire en vers," comic tales in verse, 30), which is so thoroughly ingrained that it may by now shape the thinking even of many critics who consciously reject it. No one accepts his definition as conclusive, everyone has something to add or to alter, but we continue to quote him and take him as a point of departure. There is hardly a study of the fabliaux that does not use his definition in one way or another.

Even if we are able to leave Bédier aside, serious problems remain. We should note from the outset that the question we must answer is double: what did authors mean by the word "fabliau"? and what texts are we to *count* as fabliaux? These are related questions, of course, but the relationship is by no means as close as it might appear. And it is just that connection that can cause some of the difficulty.

Philippe Ménard, in his *Les Fabliaux: contes à rire du moyen âge*, simply decides not to worry about the meaning of "fabliaux," although it is not clear how he can write a book about the fabliaux without doing so—and, of course, his generic presuppositions are evident on every page, at least by implication.[9] But he also makes a revealing comment about the problem of defining fabliaux; he points out (p. 35) that we cannot properly define the genre without studying in detail every text that belongs to it, and he is in theory correct, but in fact we clearly cannot determine which texts *do* belong to it unless we first define the genre. And here is the circularity that confronts any critic who dares talk about genre; in order to decide what

---

[8] See Hermann Schäfer, *Über die Pariser Hss. 1451 und 22555 der Huon de Bordeaux-Sage: Beziehung der Hs. 1451 zur "Chanson de Croissant"; die "Chanson de Huon et Callisse"; die "Chanson de Huon, roi de Féerie"* (Marburg: Elwert, 1892).

[9] (Paris, PUF, 1983), pp. 10, 33-37. Ménard rejects the validity of basing a definition on *fabliaux certifiés* and quotes Bédier's definition with some sympathy, but he refrains from offering a precise definition, noting that the genre is too complex and diverse to permit that. By implication, his definition appears to be "stories that most people agree are fabliaux."

fabliaux *are*, we construct a model out of texts we already *consider* to be fabliaux. If this circularity may sometimes be ignored or circumvented in practice, no one has, to my knowledge, managed to resolve it in theory.

A good many critics have attempted to define the genre in terms of self-nominated fabliaux, those that are designated as fabliaux by their own authors, or by scribes. Jodogne, Ménard (in spite of his disclaimer), Noomen, and others do so.[10] The assumption is, of course, that while works not called fabliaux may or may not be fabliaux, those so designated by the author certainly *are*, and it is from them that we can derive the characteristics of the genre. Presumably, the characteristics thus isolated could then help us identify as fabliaux a certain number of texts not so-called.[11]

Although the logic of such an approach might appear unassailable, the presupposition underlying it presents certain problems. First, it attributes to medieval authors a generic precision that the study of texts themselves does not confirm: it is far from certain that authors really know the difference, assuming there is one, between fabliaux and *dits, contes, exemples*, fables, and so on.[12] The fact that a number of the works that call themselves fabliaux also describe themselves as something else as well (either in another manuscript or in the same one) throws into doubt the assumption that the genre was sharply defined. Moreover, it is difficult to know how we might determine that a particular poem that calls itself both a fabliau and a *dit* is one instead of the other—or whether it is both. This is a problem that

---

[10] Per Nykrog, *Les Fabliaux* (Copenhagen: Munksgaard, 1957; new ed., Geneva: Droz, 1973) ; Omer Jodogne, "Le Fabliau" in *Le Fabliau et le lai narratif*, Fasc. 13 of *Typologie des Sources du Moyen Age Occidental* (Turnhout, 1975). For Noomen, see below, n. 11.

[11] As Noomen does; note that he refers to about seventy self-nominated fabliaux, but that his list, preceding the new edition, includes 127. See Willem Noomen, "Qu'est-ce qu'un fabliau?," in *Atti* of the XIV congresso internazionale di linguistica e filologia romanza, Napoli, 15-20 Aprile 1974 (Naples, 1981), pp. 421-32; Willem Noomen and Nico van den Boogaard, eds., *Nouveau Recueil complet des fabliaux*, vols. 1-6, (Assen, 1983-).

[12] As Zumthor points out, Jauss suggests that, for a brief period after 1200, *estoire* and *dit* were distinguished from "fabliau" and "fable" on the basis of their truth content. See *Essai*, p. 159.

Noomen sidesteps in his article "Qu'est-ce qu'un fabliau?," pointing out only that "fabliau" and "lai" appear to be mutually exclusive designations.[13] As for the other terms, he lists them and then ignores them.

The first problem attending such an approach is thus our inability to know just how concrete and definite might have been the generic consciousness of the medieval author.[14] To complicate matters further, we must consider at least the possibility that an author, if he did have a specific conception of genre, might intentionally misname a text for a particular purpose. That certainly happened in one direction, as when the author of *La Borgoise d'Orliens* calls it an *aventure assez cortoise*. I have elsewhere suggested that such a misnaming might contribute significantly to the comedy of a text, as the author establishes and then violates a generic "contract" with his audience.[15] Although it is less easy to demonstrate that the poet might intentionally call a non-fabliau a fabliau, we cannot know with certainty that he would not do so. In any event, authors (of whatever period) are rarely reliable guides to the study of their works, either in terms of interpretation or generic identification.

There is, as I implied earlier, yet another difficulty, and perhaps the major one. As Clayton Koelb has noted,[16] we may be talking about two entirely distinct matters when we deal with generic terminology. On the one hand, there is lexicography, the study of what a term may have meant at a certain time or to a certain author;

---

[13] Noomen, p. 431.

[14] It should be noted, however, that there appear to be certain signals that indicate that a particular composition will be a fabliau. The most intriguing suggestion about these signals was made by Keith Busby, who speculates that the attribution of a text to an author named "Garin"—the name is attached to a good number of fabliaux and even to different versions of the same story—may be an indication to the audience that they are about to hear or read a fabliau. See Busby, "Courtly Literature and the Fabliaux," p. 71.

[15] "Types of Esthetic Distance in the Fabliaux," in *The Humor of the Fabliaux: A Collection of Critical Essays*, ed. Thomas D. Cooke and Benjamin L. Honeycutt, (Columbia: University of Missouri Press, 1974), pp. 109-10.

[16] "Some Problems of Literary Taxonomy," *Canadian Review of Comparative Literature* (Autumn 1977), 235-38.

on the other, there is the critical question concerning what texts we are going to designate as fabliaux. If these two questions are not always mutually exclusive, they are certainly not identical, and perhaps not even complementary. Trying to discover just what the thirteenth century meant by "fabliau" may appear to be the proper and reasonable question, but it can in fact confuse the issue and distract us from functioning as critics and making basic judgments about literary taxonomy. The fact that authors of fabliaux themselves used generic labels indicates not that those designations were necessarily accurate or valid, but only that the Middle Ages, despite the apparent vagueness of taxonomic consciousness, shared our need to categorize, label, and compare. Not only may medieval usage have been imprecise, but it is of limited if any use in our attempts to understand what texts resemble each other sufficiently, and in what ways, to be studied together.

The validity of using self-nominated fabliaux as the basis for taxonomic considerations is called into question not only by the distinction proposed by Koelb, but also by Noomen's own study, for he is obliged to describe a dozen of the seventy works in question as "fabliaux impropres" ("Qu'est-ce qu'un fabliau?," p. 427), works that call themselves fabliaux but are not really, or at least not entirely. Such a qualification casts considerable doubt on the reliability of self-nomination: if nearly twenty percent of the authors are acknowledged to be, at best, only partially right about their own works, we cannot be entirely confident about the others. If the authors of such works as *Le Songe d'Enfer* and *De lupo et ariete* had not called them fabliaux (see Nykrog, p. 10), no one would be likely to suspect them. Furthermore, the list of self-nominated fabliaux includes a good many that, by any measure, resemble one another less closely than do a good number of other poems. For example, were it not for the single word "fablel" in a single poem from Marie's *Isopet*, Noomen would certainly not have given any attention to that text, or else he would have given equal attention to dozens, if not all, of them. He would doubtless have noted first a work like *De Vidua*, a close analogue of a self-nominated fabliau, *Cele qui se fist foutre sur la fosse de son mari*.

But if self-nomination is not a reliable basis for generic decisions, we must either find another basis for them or else discard them entirely. Some possible points of departure may be found in a consideration of subject matter, of intent, of the external shape of the work. In fact, however, most of these approaches will prove to be of little help in establishing the fabliau corpus.

One example of such a method is offered by Alfred Ewert, who insists, as noted above, that Marie de France's *Equitan* is not what he calls a *"mere* fabliau" (my emphasis).[17] In explanation, he insists that Marie is concerned principally with the analysis of feelings. Even if we acknowledge that such an analysis is not the primary concern of fabliau authors and that they expend comparatively little time and effort on it, the distinction is at best a matter of degree. *Equitan*, which concludes its "analysis of feelings" with a fine example of physical comedy illustrating the notion of duper duped, should not be casually dismissed from a discussion of fabliaux.

The lai offers the story of Equitan and his lady, who plot to scald her husband in a vat of boiling water ostensibly prepared for a bath. On the fateful day, Equitan and his lady are indulging their desires while awaiting the seneschal; he bursts into the room unannounced and finds them together. In his embarrassment, the naked Equitan leaps head first into the vat and dies, and the seneschal throws his wife into the scalding water and kills her as well.

From this summary, one would be hard-pressed to distinguish *Equitan* from a "mere" fabliau. Of course, that statement is no refutation of Ewert, who did not deny the similarity of the work's *action* to that of a fabliau. Instead, he suggested that the long discussions of the characters' reactions and emotions predominate and displace the action as primary focus, giving us a text that, being a lai, cannot be—and is not—a fabliau.

Yet, even if we concur that the analysis of feelings is the heart of this composition, there can be little reason to exclude *Equitan* from the fabliau corpus unless we also exclude a work like *La Veuve*, a composition identified, as we have seen, by some scholars as a *tableau de moeurs*, in which the action is reduced to a minimum in order to describe the reactions or desires of the widow. Moreover, we cannot so easily disregard the "fabliau-like" action and the general tone of *Equitan*, which are such that few readers, unless told otherwise, would consider the poem to be a pretext for psychological analysis. In other words, discounting the action, the tone, and the

---

[17] Alfred Ewert, ed., *Lais*, by Marie de France (Oxford: Blackwell, 1969), p. 168.

fundamental character of the work, Ewert bases his judgment solely on Marie's supposed interest in feelings—perhaps in an attempt to make this poem resemble her others.

Nor can we reasonably base our definition on suppositions about the degree of humor or the degree of moralizing offered by a work. It is by no means obvious that the humor is more important than the moralizing infent in such compositions as the *Lai d'Aristote*, *Du Vilain qui conquist paradis par plait*, or *Le preudome qui rescolt son compere de noier*; yet these texts, despite their "serious" point, have most often been considered fabliaux. Similarly unclear is the distinction between the moralizing of *Le Preudome qui rescolt son compere de noier*, usually accepted as a fabliau, and that of *La Housse partie*, often excluded from the corpus. Subjective judgments about how comic or how serious a work is can lead only to endless contradictions and critical anarchy.

Finally, we must also question the exclusion, on the grounds that only one such text calls itself a fabliau, of works inserted into collections, from the *Isopets* to Marie's lais to the *Disciplina clericalis*. From every point of view except self-nomination, a number of these stories are indistinguishable for the acknowledged fabliaux. For that matter, even the exclusion of works in prose appears to be an artificial distinction; it is a distinction we would surely not make in regard to the romance, in which the verse and prose compositions are considered variant forms, with definite historical and aesthetic implications, but by no means distinct genres.

Whereas I may appear to be destroying a useful and accepted generic label without replacing it by anything concrete, I believe there is good reason to expand the borders of the form. The label and the distinctions that go with it appear to be misleading and critically indefensible, and they are certainly more damaging than useful. They confine us to the study of an artificially limited number of texts, thereby excluding a large number that may be very similar and the study of which would be quite revealing. Critics need to be studying themes, techniques, forms in medieval short fiction, rather than limiting themselves to a group of seventy or 140 specific texts chosen not because they resemble each other internally, but because they all contain a single work or, at best, share a single characteristic.

What, then, is a fabliau—if it is anything? I once suggested that the modern form most closely related to the fabliau is the joke.[18] I would still defend that position, but with an important reservation: we can take the joke as a close relative of the fabliau, but not as its equivalent, because that too would assume that humor is the single necessary ingredient. An acceptable synonym of "fabliau" may instead be "anecdote," for the term suggests the restricted form and content, while allowing for a range of intents and effects, from bawdy humor to amusing portraits and even, conceivably, to moral lessons. Rychner also offered a definition that has much to commend it: "de bonnes histoires à servir après le repas."[19] The generality of that definition, or of the synonyms "anecdote" or simply "story" or "short narrative intended for diversion," may appear to be their weakness, but is in fact their virtue. If there is indeed a fabliau genre, it is clearly not definable with absolute precision, and our definition should reflect that generality. Humor may not be an essential component, but entertainment, in a broader sense, is; the shift of emphasis suggested here, and in Rychner's definition, will let us include a number of engaging and diverting texts that are not primarily comic and that may even contain a degree of moralizing.

We can isolate other characteristics of the form, provided we *recognize* them as characteristics, and not as criteria on which we can construct a rigid definition. For example, as various critics have suggested, the comparative brevity and narrative simplicity of works contribute in important ways to the intended effect. Although not all fabliaux limit themselves to a single action, they do consist, at least, of closely related actions occurring within a restricted period of time. Brevity, temporal compression or delimitation, and economy of narration are thus important considerations, although these too are relative matters, for they may not enable us to distinguish a long fabliau from a short romance, or any fabliau from a lai or a *conte*. Brevity imposes other demands, including the scarcity of details concerning identity, geography, psychology; in short, all the details

---

[18] In a presentation for the Symposium on Medieval Laughter, University of Southern California, Los Angeles, March 1983.

[19] "Good stories to serve after meals"; see his "Les Fabliaux: genre, styles, publics," in *La Littérature narrative d'imagination* (Paris, 1961), p. 51.

whose *absence* contributes importantly to the comic or other effect sought by authors of short narratives.[20]

Finally, there is clearly a level of style, a register, appropriate to the fabliaux. If, as Noomen suggested, the fabliau and the lai really are mutually exclusive forms, it is in part because of style and tone—except when the fabliau assumes a high style or a courtly tone for comic or parodic purposes.[21] Although Jodogne's definition of fabliaux is awkward and open to question on more than one point, his

---

[20] On this subject, see Paul Zumthor, "La Brièveté comme forme," in *Genèse, codification et rayonnement d'un genre médiéval: la nouvelle*, ed. Michaelangelo Picone, Giuseppe De Stefano, and Pamela D. Stewart (Montreal: Plato Academic Press, 1983), pp. 3-8.

[21] Even *Equitan*, the most fabliau-like of Marie's *Lais*, makes extensive use of a register that is characteristic of courtly romance. See, for example, lines 51-60 (Ewert edition):

Mut la trova curteise e sage,
Bele de cors e de visage,
De bel semblant e enveisie;
Amurs l'ad mis a sa maisnie.
Une s(e)ete ad vers lui traite,
Que mut grant plaie li ad faite,
El quor li ad lancie e mise;
N'i ad mestier sens ne cointise;
pur la dame l'ad si suspris
Tut en est murnes e pensis.

("He found her very courtly and wise, beautiful of body and face, attractive and appealing; Love gave him a place in her ranks. She shot toward him an arrow which wounded him deeply; she shot and imbedded it in his heart; wisdom and understanding were of no use in this matter; she took him by surprise through the lady, and he remained sad and pensive.")

We should note, however, that even the distinction between the styles or *registres* of fabliaux and of lais is blurred at the edges of the genres. In a composition like *Du Chevalier qui recovra l'amor de sa dame*, a work generally accepted as a fabliau, although it deals with knights, ladies, and a tourney, we would be hard-pressed to distinguish some of the language that presents the protagonist's love for a woman from that of Equitan or other "courtly" texts: "Cil chevalier voloit s'amie / Faire d'une dame, et grant poine / Sofroit por lui qu'el fust certaine / Que il l'amoit . . ." ("The knight wanted a lady for his mistress, and so that she would be certain he loved her, he took great pains . . . ," 6-9). See Chapter IV.

reference to their *ton trivial* may identify an important characteristic of the genre.[22]

Thus, a workable definition of a fabliau might be: a brief narrative text composed in a low or middle style and intended for amusement. That is not far removed, at least in spirit, from Rychner's definition, quoted above. But by expanding generic boundaries, it also raises the question of the relationship of the fabliaux to other forms, and especially to the *conte* or *nouvelle*. In fact, there is neither theoretical justification for nor practical utility in the distinction of fabliau and *nouvelle* except, perhaps, as a simple fact of literary history or chronology; we might with justification speak simply of "short narrative" (or *Kurzerzählung*, the term used by Tiemann and endorsed by Zumthor).[23] This suggestion has the disadvantage of complicating study of the fabliaux, because it expands the corpus considerably (although we do not seem to object to similar expansion in the romance form); but it may enable us to forget a number of quibbles and talk about such essential matters as *how texts work*. The narrative economy, the desire to entertain, the necessity for the *mot juste*, in some cases the comic techniques—these are shared by a considerable number of works that call themselves fabliaux and also by a considerable number that do not. Further distinctions, with the possible exception of chronological ones, appear to be pointless, unprovable, and ultimately groundless.

Finally, it might be suggested that traditional approaches to the generic question pay insufficient attention to the periphery of the genre; that is, we should not neglect works that are somewhat unlike those of our central corpus, and we should not necessarily consider them quirks. It is perhaps not those works that are anomalous, but

---

[22] Jodogne, p. 23. His complete definition is "un conte en vers où, sur un ton trivial, sont narrées une ou plusieurs aventures plaisantes ou exemplaires, l'un et l'autre ou l'un ou l'autre" ("a verse narrative presenting, in a familiar style, one or several adventures that are amusing or exemplary or both").

[23] See H. Tiemann, *Die Entstehung der mittelalterlichen Novell in Frankreich* (Hamburg, 1961). The term, as Zumthor remarks, designates "un ensemble générique cohérent"; see *Genèse, codification et rayonnement*, p. 7. It is significant that the essays in the latter volume deal not only with the *nouvelle* as a specific genre, but also with *lais*, fabliaux, and other forms, thereby supporting the contention that they are all variants of Zumthor's "ensemble générique cohérent"—the short narrative.

rather our conception of genre itself. Whereas we tend to think of genres as containing entities, into which works somehow either "fit" or do not fit, perhaps we should define literature, in terms of its various forms, as a continuum, with works distributed across its entire length but clustered more or less heavily at certain sections. Instead of "genre," the appropriate notion, at least for medieval literature, may be that of a "nexus," a group of texts that resemble each other rather closely without excluding others. Their resemblance may be ultimately less important than the extension of taxonomic boundaries to include other, less similar, texts. As experiences with the epic or the romance will show, the study of works situated on the periphery of a form is often both intrinsically valuable and practically instructive for an understanding of the very form on the periphery of which it is located.

Moreover, once we study the peripheral texts, we often find that it was nothing more than critical prejudice that ever identified them as peripheral. Chrétien de Troyes is taken, and justly so, as the finest French writer of romance, but once we devote sufficient attention to other romances, we cease to assume that *only* a work by Chrétien can serve as an adequate model for the genre. The result is that our conception of genre, and indeed of literature, becomes less narrow and parochial. There is clearly *practical* value in imposing narrower generic boundaries—editions of fabliaux, for example, must have some limits—but we should accept those limits as a practical necessity and convenience, not as a critical reality.

In conclusion, the problem may be less our understanding of the word "fabliau" than our understanding of genre itself. I am not suggesting that we purge our critical vocabulary of the term "fabliau": we need taxonomic distinctions, and if we stop calling these works "fabliaux," we will start calling them something else. The reader may find it ironic that, having devoted a number of pages to definitional matters and in particular to the uncertainty of generic designations, I will continue in the ensuing chapters to use the term "fabliau" routinely. In fact, having resisted the urge to open this chapter with an analysis of a lai (e.g., *Equitan*) or other "non-fabliau," I will for the most part continue unapologetically to follow conventional practice in the choice of texts to be discussed. Almost without exception, those texts are "mainstream," typical fabliaux, routinely recognized as such by scholars.[24]

That, I hope, will not be taken as an indication that the preceding discussion of taxonomic problems has been pointless. Not only are my observations crucial as a matter of theory, but they have practical implications as well: they will preclude any assumptions on my part and perhaps on the reader's that texts that are called fabliaux must or do share certain characteristics or values. And if we continue to talk of fabliaux or any other form, we should recognize that our terminology is no more than a convention, capable sometimes of facilitating, but just as often impeding, our understanding of texts. Only if we acknowledge the fragility of medieval categories and terms can we begin to focus our critical attention properly, not on an artificially limited group of texts, but on the methods and materials of short narrative fiction. And, manifestly, the methods of composing short fictional texts do not necessarily vary with the labels given them either by their authors or by us.

---

[24] One of the few exceptions, located on the periphery of the genre, is the text that opens this chapter: *La Veuve*. In addition to *Equitan*, I also refer briefly to *Audigier* in Chapter VI.

III. The Conservatism of the Fabliaux

Text: *Du vilain asnier*

51 lines
MR, V, 40-42

[A peasant who customarily uses his donkeys to transport manure finds himself one day in a street occupied by spice merchants; he faints from the odor. Passersby think him dead until a preudome *arrives and announces that he can revive the peasant. He does so by holding manure before the unconscious man's nose. When the smell supplants that of the herbs and spices, the peasant awakens and pronounces himself cured. He swears never to come that way again. The moral is that one should remain in one's element.]*

Although most of my chapters begin with a close reading of a full fabliau text, I am intentionally opening this one with a short composition concerning which there might appear to be little commentary necessary or even possible. The fact is, however, that this composition, even though it is one of the simpler fabliaux, offers us one of the most fundamental and revealing insights into the ethos of these works.

Many fabliaux concern *vilains*. The word means "peasants" but very often refers to character and social context as well as economic status[1]: *vilain* is clearly and systematically contrasted to *courtois*

---

[1] In fact, the word *vilain* does not always imply poverty; the *Vilain qui conquist paradis par plait* says that the *vilain*—and it is a word used almost a dozen times in the brief text—had given food, lodging, clothing, and comfort to the poor. On the other hand, the association of the term *vilain* with ignoble character is made explicitly in *Des chevaliers, des deus clercs, et les villains*: "nus n'est vilains se de cuer non: / vilains est qui fet vilonie, / ja tant n'ert de haute lingnie!" ("it is one's heart that makes one ignoble [*vilain*]: he who commits ignoble acts is ignoble, no matter how noble his birth").

("courtly") and, as in this text, to *preudome* indicating a worthy or noble man, a man of experience and means, a man of the world. *Vilains* are most often base and crude, though not necessarily evil. The fabliaux generally reveal an anti-*vilain* bias: peasants are simply foreign to the bourgeois/clerical center out of which most often comes the point of view of fabliau authors.[2]

Du vilain asnier plays, more effectively than most fabliaux, on the contrast between peasants and "others" in order to teach a conservative lesson through humor that certainly would have appealed to fabliau audiences. That which "we" find pleasant and appealing, the scent of spices and herbs, is powerfully destructive to peasants, more properly accustomed to the smell of manure.

The text initially has about it the scent, as it were, of the kind of "topsy-turvy" world popular in medieval literature, a world where everything is the precise opposite of what is expected. In such a context, manure would be pleasant, the smell of spices odious. That, of course, proves to be an incorrect interpretation, and it is quickly clear that the odor of manure is not necessarily pleasing, but merely familiar and appropriate, because it *belongs* to the world inhabited by peasants.

Thus, the peasant responds favorably to that odor because he is accustomed to it (see 2-4: ". . . estoit costumier / De fiens chargier et amasser / A .II. asnes terre fumer") and, to put it more directly, because he is a peasant. Had we any doubt about this, it would surely be resolved by the fact that it is specifically a *preudome* who understands what has occurred and who is thus able to revive him and, more important, teach him a valuable lesson. That lesson, should doubt still remain, is made explicit in the moral of the story: ". . . cil fait ne sens ne mesure / Qui d'orgueil se desennature: / *Ne se doit nus desnaturer*" ("he who, because of pride, finds himself out of his element is neither wise nor prudent; no one should abandon his nature," 49-51). The *Vilain asnier* is thus a lesson in class segregation: even *vilains* themselves are far better off if they "keep to their own," if they do not mingle with *preudomes*. The moral thus cautions us that it is not good to be out of one's element.

---

[2] An exception, again, is the *Vilain qui conquist paradis par plait*, which repeatedly demonstrates not only the sly and quick wit of a *vilain*, but also his moral superiority over the saints.

It is important, however, that we not overlook the lines preceding the moral. They tell us that the ideals of *sens* ("wisdom" or sensibleness) and *mesure*, meaning "moderation," "proportion," or "propriety,"[3] are negated when anyone *se desennature* (fails to respect his nature or station). More important still is the narrator's explanation of the cause for such an offense: *orgueil* ("pride").

Readers may find that explanation surprising, since there is no overt indication in the text that the peasant suffered from pride; nor are we told that he had the least desire to become, or become like, the *preudome*. In fact, however, this is simply a matter of definition: the man's actions *constitute* pride, irrespective of his intention. Pride implies excess and pretention, and for the author of this fabliau those vices are linked to acts and events, not necessarily, as we might assume, to character and motivation. Thus, the *asnier*'s presence in a street of spice merchants is simply, in the ethos of this genre, wrong.

The narrator has juxtaposed incongruous elements. Peasants and *preudomes* are oil and water. They simply do not mix, and the inevitable result of their encounter is harm to the lower of the classes. This is the usual perspective of class conservatism: "they" may be in an inferior position, but they are in reality better off staying there. Not only is it *proper* for the ass-driver to avoid the spice merchants, but he is the better off for doing so.

*

The fabliaux generally indulge in humor and fun at the expense not only of ignorant peasants, but also of jealous and stupid husbands, lascivious priests, libidinous and insatiable women, and the occasional fallen philosopher. Their authors, in fact, are consistently irreverent, seeming to take nothing seriously and considering practically nothing sacred. It would be easy—but erroneous—to equate this irreverent spirit with subversion. Instead, the fabliaux as a group are profoundly conservative, even reactionary, compositions, using humor to preserve and enforce a status quo considered to be natural

---

[3] The wife in *Le Chevalier qui fist sa fame confesse* refers explicitly to households that are "sanz mesure" ("unnatural" or "improper," 207), by which she means households in which the woman is dominant.

or even divinely instituted. In other words, these ostensibly marginal texts assume the propriety of the established social order and the wisdom of the idea that one should be satisfied with whatever one has or is.

La Pucele qui voloit voler concerns a young woman who one day simply decides that she wants to be able to fly. A cleric offers to assist her by constructing a beak and tail. The former consists of more than thirty kisses (38-40). The latter can be accomplished only by copulation, which is described briefly but crudely (48-49). But he then explains to her that making a tail requires a full year of patient labor, which he is willing to contribute. He continues to assist her each day, and eventually she becomes pregnant.

This fabliau belongs to a group in which euphemisms are exploited to seduce a woman, naive or not,[4] but it is of particular interest here because of the narrator's explicit condemnation of the young woman's desire to fly: it is *grant desmesure* ("inordinate" or unrealistic; see 98 and 107) and *otrage* ("outrage," 105). As a result, she has no one but herself to blame for her plight: "Qui otrage quiert il li vient" ("whoever seeks an outrage receives it," 105). Thus does the fabliau denounce the young woman's pretentions in wanting to fly and suggests that her defloration and pregnancy are an appropriate way to deflate those pretentions and punish her for them.

In fact, the very beginning of the text had offered a key to the narrator's view. We are told that the young woman is beautiful and thus is sought by numerous suitors—clerics, knights, bourgeois, and squires—but accepts none of them. After that introduction to her, the narrator bluntly notes, entirely without explanation, that "one day she announced that she would like to fly" (10). The juxtaposition of those passages implies their equivalence; it suggests that the desire to fly, or conceivably any other unrealistic ambition, is a mere extension of her haughty disdain for her suitors. That is, by refusing to marry, she is displaying behavior that is as inappropriate, as outlandish, as would be a desire to fly. It is, in other words, contrary to nature, and the fabliaux almost invariably react to such unnatural acts by setting the situation right and punishing those who commit such acts, whether it has been done by accident (as with the *vilain asnier*) or arrogance (the woman who wished to fly). The fabliaux may or may not have a

---

[4] See Chapter VI.

didactic intent in regard to their audience, but their characters, at
least, often do learn lessons.

Frere Denise has much in common, ideologically if not
narratively, with *La Pucele qui voloit voler*. Denise is a young
noblewoman who wants to enter religious orders; she is assisted by
Brother Simon, a Franciscan whose interests go beyond the pious and
who agrees to accept her, properly disguised, into his community.
Eventually, a *châtelaine* sees her and realizes that she is a woman,
whereas the other brothers had not. This *châtelaine* berates Denise
for her *folie* (220) and viciously attacks religious hypocrisy; she
reconciles Denise with her mother and respects the young woman's
secret.

This is a rather complex fabliau. Ostensibly, it sets out to
illustrate the proverb "Li abiz ne fait pas l'ermite" ("the habit does
not make the hermit," or "clothes do not make the man," 1), but that
proverb is applicable both to Denise and to Brother Simon, for his
motives were far from the purity demanded by the narrator (1-13).
Moreover, Denise had already taken an oath of chastity "a Deu et a
Notre Dame" (26-27), and the implication is clearly that it is a short
step from her oath to a life that, at least theoretically, incarnates just
such an ideal of chastity. If thereafter the religious life is shown to be
folie for her, the further implication is that her original oath was
wrong—but that is a point to which we shall return.

Simon insists that she can enter his order only if she wishes to
retain her virginity forever. She accepts the invitation (66-68), but
before long Simon has his way with her and teaches her some "new
games" (164). Her entry into religion, being fraudulent, destroys
precisely that which she entered it to preserve, and the Franciscan is
at fault.

But, in fact, the fault is not his alone. She too is at fault, not
only because of her entry into religious orders, but ultimately because
of the inclinations that caused her to seek and accept such a role.
The key details are her initial oath of chastity and its consequence:
she had refused more than twenty marriage proposals from fine men
(22-25). There can be no doubt whatsoever that the narrator takes
that to be improper if not incomprehensible behavior by a courtly
young woman.

If that is so, then the ensuing events are morally complex:
Simon's actions are hypocritical, and his hypocrisy is duly punished,

but those same actions serve as a necessary corrective for Denise's *folie*. And at this point we see that her folly was double: she was foolish to enter a masculine order, but even earlier she had been equally foolish to reject the kind of life a courtly lady should have sought or, at least, accepted. The proof is that once she has learned her lesson and been reunited with her mother, she dutifully marries one of the men she had earlier rejected, and thereafter she enjoys great honor.

Again, if her becoming a Franciscan brother is wrong, it is apparent that her initial rejection of men and marriage is considered an unnatural act, and in the fabliaux unnatural acts must be corrected. Propriety must be respected and, where it is lacking, reinstituted. Like *La Pucele qui voloit voler*, this text depicts a woman who wants something that, in the conservative world of the fabliaux, a woman should not want. The text restores equilibrium and teaches the woman a lesson. In *La Pucele qui voloit voler*, this involves punishment and humiliation for the young woman; in *Frere Denise*, she loses her chastity, but her honor is ultimately maintained and she is finally better, not worse, off. That the lessons are taught by, respectively, a lecherous cleric and a hypocritical Franciscan is not without interest: they themselves may be beneath contempt, but their actions have definite utility. They deflate what the authors consider female pretentions and restore a proper equilibrium in human society and, there can be no doubt, in God's plan for the world.

An important, but by no means surprising, aspect of fabliau conservatism concerns the "proper" relationship of woman to man, specifically of wife to husband. That is the subject of much of Chapter V, and I thus risk repeating myself once too often. Yet the importance of preordained roles in the fabliaux is such that the risk is justified, especially when those roles are not only imposed by the narrator but are presumably reflective, as I indicated above, of certain medieval notions about "God's plan."

Sire Hain et Dame Anieuse offers one of the least subtle developments of this theme. The couple decide to settle their considerable marital differences with fisticuffs, with the winner earning the right to wear the pants—literally: the man's *braies* are placed on the ground, where they are to be taken by the victor. Sire Hain beats and humiliates Anieuse, and she, who had habitually defied her husband, must now swear to obey him, *"as a worthy woman ought to do"* ("si com preude fame doit fere," 379, my emphasis). In fact, she never again contradicts him, because she "feared his blows" (398). The moral of the story explicitly endorses physical violence against any wife who is arrogant (404) and "disdains" her husband (410).

It should be emphasized here that neither this fabliau nor any other that exploits the same theme is suggesting that "might makes right," that is, that the man deserves respect and the woman should be subservient simply because he is the stronger. Rather, his greater strength is simply the instrumentality by which he is able to enforce or restore a relationship between the sexes that is considered intrinsically proper.

In fact, the number of fabliaux that treat this theme confirms that fabliau authors simply assumed the propriety, the naturalness, of masculine superiority. Women's subjugation, often identified as "respect" for her husband, should be maintained, and physical force, where needed, is endorsed as a methodology. The only fabliau more brutal than *Sire Hain* in this regard may be *De la dame escolliee*, analyzed in detail in Chapter V. That composition shows graphically what happens when the proper (which is to say natural) place of man and woman is reversed. Its moral, reactionary in the extreme, concerns women who hate or subjugate men, but the hatred or scorn derives from, and is virtually synonymous with, their being placed above men. In such instances, of course, men share in the blame, even if the narrator chooses not to assign it to them: they cede the ascendancy to women and thus father that scorn. Other fabliaux, as Chapter V will show, deal with a single aspect of woman's presumptuousness, such as the impropriety of her being sexually dominant (see, in this regard, my later discussion of *La Dame qui aveine demandoit pour Morel sa provende avoir* and of *Porcelet*).

But it would be wrong to assume that fabliaux deal in uniform manner with this or any other subject. Most often, it is true, the conclusion of the text restores the appropriate balance between the sexes, meaning that it reduces the woman to subservience. There are a number of exceptions, however. *Le Chevalier qui fist sa fame confesse*, for example, permits the quick-thinking wife to evade punishment for her offenses and, presumably, to continue to indulge her insatiable sexual appetite.

Yet, although the conclusion of that story may be atypical, the text, in the words of the woman herself, agrees with other fabliaux about the "place" of woman and the destructive effect of her domineering way. The woman in *Le chevalier qui fist sa fame confesse*, thinking that she is dying, confesses that she had reduced her husband to nothing. She further notes, in words that surely reflect the narrator's sentiments, that "ne ja ostel n'ert a honor / Dont la dame se fet seignor" ("No household has honor if the lady makes herself its lord," 201-02), and she concludes that it is women's nature to dominate men (203-08).

Here is a curious contradiction, attested by numerous fabliaux: whereas it is nature's plan for man to dominate woman, it is woman's nature to dominate man. It requires no great subtlety to complete the syllogism: the character of woman is therefore contrary to nature. The inevitable result is a war between the sexes played out through a good many fabliaux, with the nearly inevitable and clearly conservative outcome being the victory of the male and the return of the female to her proper subservience.

Even as silly a fabliau as *La Couille noire* is conservative in its own way. The woman, surprised and indignant when she observes that her husband's genitals are black, tries to divorce him and is punished for her impudence; the moral insists that she should have been satisfied with what she had, rather than try to change the situation. This moral, however, adds a small detail and thereby suggests, not that one should resign oneself to something inferior, but rather that one should be content, because whatever one has is as good as the alternative: in life as, presumably, in genital color, black is as good as white (120-21). If the fabliau suggests that the grass always appears greener (or the genitals whiter) on the other side of the fence, it also demonstrates that appearances are deceiving: the grass on this side is just as good. Whence the conservatism of the text: be content. Do not want what you do not have.

The narrator of *Les Putains et les lecheors* opens his story by telling us that when God created the world, He established three orders of people: clerics, knights, and laborers. But God had forgotten something: He had also created prostitutes and jongleurs and had neglected to provide for them. He rectifies that oversight by entrusting prostitutes to clerics and jongleurs to knights. But unfortunately, says the jongleur who is telling this story, only the clerics discharge their duties properly, giving to prostitutes fine food, rich clothes, and their company in bed. Knights, on the other hand, are avaricious and stingy, offering to jongleurs only the few crumbs necessary to keep them alive.

This text strikes with cuttingly ironic praise at clerics, who earn their salvation by enthusiastically obeying God's order to care for prostitutes; it also indicts those who fail to care properly for jongleurs ("Et li chevalier sont dampné," 82). But although the narrator's intent may be jocular, his assumptions are revealing: to his mind, the social order has a divinely established origin. Not only did God establish social classes, but He further determined the conditions of their existence: knights would live from their lands, clerics from tithes and offerings, and laborers from the sweat of their brow (". . . asena les laborages / As laboranz por laborer," 10-11). Thus, things and people in the world are fundamentally in the place God has established for them. What more conservative, even reactionary, attitude than to contend that laborers labor *because God wants them to?*[5] In its narratorial attitudes, this text is not far removed from *Du vilain asnier*: if your job is to haul manure, avoid the spice merchants.

In the traditional contrast between nature and nurture, the conservative fabliaux consistently endorse the former and imply, furthermore, that nurture contains more than a fair measure of artifice. The most telling example is the *Lai d'Aristote*, in which Aristotle's pretense of detached reason, like his "unnatural" denial of appetites, is shown to be a sham when his own appetites are excited.

We might suggest further, though purely in speculation, that this preference for what is natural explains the prevalence of fabliaux involving lascivious priests. Although I see no evidence that the fabliaux criticize or condemn the church,[6] many of them appear to

---

[5] The modern equivalent, which unfortunately is not fictional, may be a prominent politician's justifying his neglect of the poor by citing the scriptural contention that the poor will always be with us. From that statement, it is only a short step to a claim that God has instituted and sanctioned poverty; the poor, thus, should be happy to be poor.

[6] As O'Gorman notes, "Let it be noted . . . that the satire directed . . . against an individual or a group of clerics is not an attack on the powers of the clergy as such—although the priest was fair game, his office was not." See Richard O'Gorman, ed. *Les Braies au Cordelier* (Birmingham: Summa, 1983), p. 7.

imply that the priesthood itself is an unnatural condition in which a man may find himself. In any contest between the priest and the man, between the cloth and the flesh, the latter wins; sexual appetites are normal, and a situation in which those appetites are supposed to be suppressed only sharpens them. That priests are so often the losers in the sexual games they play must constitute an indictment not of sexuality itself, for the narrators of fabliaux heartily endorse that, but of an institution that would deny it.

If the fabliaux develop themes that are conservative in regard to social and sexual distinctions, their linguistic resources are similarly conservative, although that may not be immediately apparent. In fact, although many fabliaux use words not admissible in decent circles, those words are themselves few, and they identify in the most direct fashion the acts and objects they designate. That short list of words includes *foutre, con, couille* and *couillon, vit, cul, chier, pisser, peter*; that largely exhausts the list. The prevalence of these unadorned nouns and verbs reflects a decided preference for maintaining a direct and simple connection between words and the things they designate. The other face of this coin is a rejection of linguistic artifice, as fabliaux often demonstrate the unacceptability of euphemism and metaphor and provide a frontal attack on the prevailing literary language.

I discuss these tendencies in detail in Chapter VI, indicating that euphemisms in particular are dangerous. Almost invariably, the refusal to call things by their ordinary names will lead directly to the precise result, usually sexual intercourse, that the euphemisms were designed to preclude, and those results, again almost invariably, prove far more salacious or violent than the "real" name could have been.

Even when sex is not involved, figurative language is often undermined or redefined literally, not only by fabliau characters but by the texts themselves. Thus, in *Brunain, la vache au prestre*, a priest who stands to profit from the scriptures preaches that whatever one gives to God, through the priest, will be doubled; a poor couple take his advice as literal precept—which may not have been contrary to his intent—and give him their cow. That advice, however, really *is* literally realized when they, not he, end up with two cows.

Whereas the morals of fabliaux may be varied and sometimes illogical, their actual "lesson" is comparatively simple and is conservative. It is difficult to think of an existing fabliau, or to conceive of a potential one, that we might take as genuinely subversive. The authors who choose this genre do not appear concerned with challenging existing institutions, except where a text has institutionalized the unnatural. On the contrary, they demonstrate that in language and conduct (sexual and otherwise), in work and ambitions and relations between social classes and between husband and wife, there is a natural order. That order should be respected and cultivated, and when it is not, the inevitable result is discord and misery for the culprit—and laughter for the reader.

Whether the conservatism of fabliaux is both reflective and corrective may be uncertain. That is, it surely reflects a common medieval view of what is natural, normal, proper, even divinely established. It may also indicate, though this is speculative, that in the thirteenth-century world, the established order was being upset and challenged to the point that one of the oldest of weapons, humor, had to be marshaled in defense of the status quo. By its nature, laughter is an instrument of prevention, correction, or retribution, but not of subversion. It is a method of deflating pretentions and deriding those who themselves attempt to subvert an assumed natural order. It is the tool of a very conservative ideology.

It is clear that the fabliaux are not the subversive texts a casual reading might imply. Quite the contrary: beneath a heavy textual veneer of seductions and infidelities, tricks and betrayals, lies and misunderstandings, and occasional murders, we find a strict and traditional social morality[7] that opts for, or at least longs for, a neat and orderly arrangement of social relationships, sexual roles, and class distinctions. This attitude sees a place for everything and would dearly like to see everything in its place. Or, as the author of *Du vilain asnier* put it, more elegantly, "ne se doit nus desnaturer."

---

[7] Jürgen Beyer contends instead that the fabliaux are "free of any concern for value." I disagree: it is true that a moral intent may not be deduced from a consideration of the "morals" appended to them; nonetheless, their almost predictable reaction against any character who diverges from what is thought appropriate and natural surely reveals the authors' assumptions (conscious or not) about "proper behavior." See Beyer's "The Morality of the Amoral," in *The Humor of the Fabliaux: A Collection of Critical Essays*, ed. Thomas D. Cooke and Benjamin L. Honeycutt (Columbia: University of Missouri Press, 1974), p. 38 and passim.

IV. Courtliness and the Fabliaux

Text: *Du chevalier qui recovra l'amor de sa dame*

By Pierre d'Alphonse (?)
254 lines
MR, VI, 138-46

[A certain knight loves a married woman. Because he has never performed any act of prowess for her, she doubts his love, and he thus proposes to organize a tournament where she might see him in action. In the tournament, he defeats her husband. Unfortunately, another knight dies in battle, and the tourney ends. The woman invites her suitor to come to her that night. When he arrives, he is informed that she will join him as soon as her husband is sleeping. While waiting, the exhausted knight falls asleep, and the lady orders her chambermaid to send him away. Informed by the maid that he has offended his lady, he approaches the bed and tells her startled husband that he is the knight killed earlier in the day and that his soul will be freed only when the wife pardons him for an offense he did her. The husband urges her to grant the request; she initially refuses, but agrees after the knight declines to reveal the nature of the offense. He goes away happy.]

The author of this work begins with a typical formula, announcing his intention to tell an *aventure* without delay. He moves quickly into the story, individualizing the context of the work only slightly, with a vague reference to time ("not long ago") and an indication of locale (Normandy). As in the majority of fabliaux, the characters are not named. Somewhat less typical is the characters' social level: we learn that the story will concern not a bourgeois or a *vilain*, but a knight and a lady.

Even though the generic identification makes use of an entirely conventional formula, the choice of terms may not be without significance in this case. It has often been noted that authors traditionally identify fabliaux by a variety of terms (fabliau, *dit*, *conte*, etc.), which frequently appear to be interchangeable and which may even vary from one manuscript to another of the same composition. Nonetheless, the use of *aventure* in the text may well be an intentional device used to create a tone in keeping with the chivalric context. Whatever the author's intention, the generality of the term *aventure* prevents the creation of the expectations that would be aroused by the word "fabliau" (which does indeed appear, but only in the conclusion).

There is nothing in the beginning of the poem, and very little throughout, to identify *Du chevalier qui recovra l'amor de sa dame* as a fabliau, at least in the usual sense of the word.[1] In fact, this is one of the fabliaux that Mary Jane Schenck would exclude from the canon, because it is, in her view, a courtly tale, a "conte courtois."[2] We are to hear an *aventure* concerning a knight and a lady; the author uses courtly expressions, telling us that the knight wants to make the lady his *amie* (6) and that he suffers for her (he endures "grant poine," 7) and does everything possible to please her. When she deigns to speak with him, she asks how he can reasonably seek her love, when he has never done "chevalerie / Ne proece" (knightly or valiant deeds, 18-19) for her. To this point, were we not reading the tale in an edition that identifies the genre as fabliau, there would be nothing to tell us that the work before us is not a lai or, were it longer, a romance. The courtly tone that has dominated the beginning of the poem continues, as the knight asks "Ma dame" to grant him permission to organize a tourney, in which she may see how "lance et escuz" (lance and shield) suit him.

When the knight prepares to organize events, the author's concern for narrative economy expresses itself in the use of a technique that we will find throughout many fabliaux and other short works. In two lines, he tells us: "En vait lo tornoiemant prandre. / Ez vos que li tornoiz est pris" ("He goes off to arrange the tournament; now the tournament is arranged," 40-41). This method, telling us that "he

---

[1] For the moment, I am intentionally neglecting the problems of fabliau terminology and of the very notion of genres in medieval literature; I have discussed those fully in Chapter II.

[2] *The Fabliaux: Tales of Wit and Deception* (Amsterdam: John Benjamins, 1987), p. 68.

prepares to do it; now it is done," is used in other fabliaux as well, to indicate physical movement, telling us, for example, that a man is to go somewhere, is on his way, is there. The technique permits the author to pass quickly over information that, while needed, would diffuse his focus if related in detail. Moreover, in the present fabliau, the poet emphasizes the foreshortening of time by concluding the two lines with forms of the same verb (the past participle of 41 indicating completion) and by the use of *Ez vos* ("voilà," "behold"), a common locution used to denote either a change of scene or the beginning or conclusion of an event. *Ez vos* recurs a few lines later (50) to announce the commencement of the tourney.[3]

Details of the tourney appear designed to emulate romance (or even epic) style: the knights, ready to do battle, don hauberks and helmets, and the lady's suitor and husband begin the action. The contest between them follows a predictable course—the suitor wins—but the poet's method deserves note. The two combatants break their lances and then continue with their swords; but then, apparently in the middle of the battle, the narrator notes that the knight who wanted to impress his lady *leaves her* (73) and goes to attack her husband. He quickly goes a certain distance away, returning to attack with a lance; his speed is indicated by a comparison more reminiscent of romance than of fabliaux: he leaves faster than a well-seated arrow flies from a bow (74-75).

It is not entirely clear whether he was near her while fighting and simply moved away to continue the battle or whether the narrator is using an iterative technique, recounting the beginning of the action a second time for emphasis; whatever the case, the reference to the lady apparently *during* the battle, rather than simply before it, reestablishes her and the knight's love for her as the focus of the work.

The author presents the conclusion of the battle by a synecdoche, a method hardly typical of fabliau styles: the knight attacks his adversary, and "breastplates and saddlegirths" ("poitraus ne cengle," 77) fall in a heap. When the woman sees what has befallen her husband, she grieves for him but is pleased by her suitor's success.

---

[3] Similarly, *De cele qui se fist foutre sur la fosse de son mari* (40) announces the change of scene and the arrival of the knight and squire by the same locution.

Fabliau authors frequently express an awareness of the necessity for brevity; in fact, not only the brevity but the explicit references to it seem to be characteristic of the genre. The present author is no exception, and after offering considerable detail about the tourney to this point, he hurries on, suggesting (84) that a prolonged story would be pointless. In only eleven lines (85-95), we learn that all the knights begin to joust, one of them is killed, everyone grieves, they bury him, and, since it is late, they then disperse. This event and the lady's subsequent invitation for the knight to visit her that night form the conclusion to the first section of the poem.

Although the death of a knight in the tournament will prove to be the key to the entire work, the function of the event is by no means clear at this point. The attentive reader who notes the almost brusque narration of the death and of the tourney's end may well take it simply as a convenient but graceless form of closure. It is closure, of course, and also transition, but it is considerably less graceless than it may seem. To dwell on it would be to magnify its importance in our minds, whereas a good part of the humorous appeal of the poem will derive from the ingenuity of the knight and from our recognition and mild surprise when his stratagem is revealed to us.

That the first portion of this bipartite poem is intended as background and preparation is indicated not only by its comparative brevity and temporal compression, but also by the fact that it consists almost entirely of narration, in the third person and with a single instance of direct discourse. By contrast, well over half the lines following the end of the tourney are taken up with dialogue (ninety lines out of 150, in fact). The first half of the composition thus consists of summary; the second half, of dramatized events.

Once the suitor arrives at her home, the pace of the story slows extraordinarily. Emphasizing the economy of fabliau narration, critics routinely, though inaccurately, contend that fabliaux typically exclude all elements inessential to the intrigue,[4] but we must at least inquire at this point about some obviously superfluous details of the story. A servant leads him to a room (112), tells him to wait, and then goes to inform her lady "Del chevalier et qu'il estoit / En la chanbre o il atendoit" ("About the knight and the fact that he was waiting in the room," 117-18); the lady announces that she will come to the knight

---

[4] See Chapter VII.

when her husband is asleep. At this point, and in the lines to come, the author does not appear particularly concerned with narrative economy: had he been, he could have saved a good deal of time by having the woman confide all her plans earlier to the servant (but not necessarily to us); the maid could then simply inform the knight that he was to wait and that his lady would arrive when her husband fell asleep. For that matter, the lady herself could have given him instructions at the tourney.

Obviously, we are now at the heart of the intrigue, and the narrator develops it dramatically, at moments slowing the time of narration very nearly to the elapsed time of events. Though the detail lavished on the scene is not required for the coherent development of the tale, the deceleration does serve a definite purpose: it not only permits the poet to prepare and develop the situation in detail, for narrative effect, but it also dramatizes the actual delay that leads the knight to fall asleep. In that sense, the detail offered by the poet is inessential but not, in terms of narrative effect, superfluous.

Furthermore, when the lady sees that a knight who would risk any danger for her (103-04) cannot even stay awake, she does not chastise him directly; declining to speak to him, she returns and orders her servant to send him away, and the poet even takes time to relate the servant's disbelief that he would commit such an offense. The pace and dialogue permit the author to present reactions directly, instead of merely summarizing actions; the resulting emphases suggest that the effectiveness of the anecdote depends in part on the presentation of character, and not merely, as we might expect in fabliaux, on the unfolding of the anecdote. Thus, although these details may not be needed for the simple narration of events, they serve a decided purpose in providing emphasis and dramatic coloring.

The leisurely pace continues, as the servant's words to the knight are reported to us. She further emphasizes the outrageous nature of his offense by pointing out the nobility and beauty of her lady, described as "si trés noble . . . / Si bele et si blanche et si tandre, / Et si vaillant" ("very noble, very beautiful and fair and tender, and very worthy," 173-75)—in short, clearly deserving of better treatment. Parenthetically, it should be noted that the description of the lady is accomplished by a very common formula used routinely to praise a lady; it is a "courtly" formula taken over, perhaps for purposes of humor or parody, by authors of fabliaux and other works. The usual description is somewhat simpler than here (e.g., "bele, cortoise et sage"), as the maid multiplies adjectives to emphasize the suitor's unworthiness.

The chagrined knight asks permission to enter the bedchamber, and the next dozen lines constitute the only significant segment of summary narrative in the second half. He expresses his desire to "do something" ("faire rien," 183) and, once in the room, approaches the bed with his sword drawn. It immediately becomes clear that he intends no physical harm, and it is at this point that the pieces of the intrigue, the puzzle, come together. He announces that he is the knight killed earlier that day (202-04) and that his soul cannot leave his body until the lady has forgiven him for a wrong he did her (206-11).

Except for the fabrication concerning his identity, the knight tells the entire truth: he has offended her, he is seeking her pardon, and he cannot reveal the nature of the offense, because that revelation would leave him far worse off than he now is (236-37). Until this last statement, the lady had refused to forgive him. Now, she appears to be doubly impressed, first by his resolve and courage in entering the room—an act of prowess ("proece") that demonstrates, better than his performance on the battlefield, the depth of his love for her—and then by his discretion, an essential quality of courtly and adulterous loves. Having had both proved to her, she relents and pardons him. She is able not only to love him, since *he* loves *her* enough to run a considerable risk for her, but to trust him as well.

Once the knight has accomplished his purpose, the story ends with a promptness that may surprise us; yet the anecdote is ended, and loose ends have been tied up. Consequently, he simply goes away. There is no need to provide details of their love or of a physical consummation—if indeed there is one: we have no right to assume that their love involves seduction and sexual attachment, or even that it has any future at all, since the text does not inform us of it.[5] In fact, the storyteller leaves us where a modern narrator probably would not: the subterfuge is successful, and nothing more is needed. Since we know that he has gained, then recovered the lady's love, the narrator does not need to tell us more. He knows when to end, pausing only to give his name, Pierres d'Anfol, and to add a simple

---

[5] On the subject of implicitness in fabliau endings, see Chapter X.

conclusion insisting on the work's didactic value as instruction ("enseignemant," 250).

*

This fabliau, neither the best-known nor the best representative of its genre, is nonetheless of interest for several reasons. In addition to the notable shift of narrative method in the middle of the work and the abundant use of dialogue thereafter, the courtly tone and milieu clearly merit discussion, and we may also look profitably at questions of the poem's generic identification, its comic "mechanism," and the function of surprise in fabliaux.

The reader acquainted with fabliau conventions and perhaps with related situations in other texts would doubtless anticipate an amusing turn of events when the man enters the bedchamber: although he enters with drawn sword, convention dictates deception rather than violence. Fabliau husbands, after all, may be roundly beaten but are rarely run through. We can also be assured that he will succeed, and this assurance raises question about the function of surprise in the fabliaux. Cooke contends that surprise is the essence of fabliau humor,[6] but we should note that the only surprises we encounter here concern the *means* by which the work will arrive at a destination that is never seriously in doubt.

That is, we cannot doubt that the knight will succeed, but we likely do not anticipate his method. The humor depends on the satisfaction of our ultimate expectations, not on their frustration,[7] and specifically on the unexpected way they are satisfied. In this text, we must also appreciate the knight's courage (as the wife clearly does) and his

---

[6] Thomas D. Cooke, *The Old French and Chaucerian Fabliaux: A Study of Their Comic Climax* (Columbia: University of Missouri Press, 1978), pp. 13-14, 53-57.

[7] See below, Chapter VIII; see also my article "The Fabliaux and Comic Logic," *L'Esprit Créateur*, 16.1 (1976), 39-45.

ingenuity as well, and we simply suspend our disbelief in regard to the husband's credulity.[8]

I have referred to this work as a fabliau. Is it one? And why? The author calls it a fabliau, but only in the conclusion, and two of the editors of the work (Johnston and Owen, p. 110) note that "this charming courtly tale is really a fabliau in little but name" and that it clearly "stands on the periphery of the genre." As I have noted, the beginning of the poem announces an *aventure*, the characters are noble, and the work presents a conventional courtly situation: a suitor's attempt to win a lady's love. Except for the failure to name and individualize the characters—a common practice of fabliaux authors—there is nothing here to create the specific expectations we would bring to a work that, for example, announced the poet's intention to tell a tale about a woman who could not bear to hear anyone "parler de foutre," that is, speak about screwing. That is precisely the point developed in my discussion of taxonomic problems: works of various kinds inevitably suffer from our imposition of rigid generic boundaries.

I am convinced, in fact, that medieval audiences had certain generic assumptions; but the value of those assumptions was related not to the specific establishment of categories and criteria, but to the more generalized creation of comic and other expectations. *Du chevalier qui recovra l'amor de sa dame*, if we can call it a fabliau, offers an example at one end of the comic spectrum: it is a short courtly tale in which a knight's conquest of a lady involves a clever and amusing stratagem. This is scarcely a salacious tale, and if it elicits a smile, it certainly does not provoke robust laughter. Yet there is another narrative fact that sets it apart from certain other stories in which a knight's persistence or courage earns him a lady's love. That is the fact that his subterfuge enables him to enlist the aid of the lady's husband as accomplice, for it is in no small part the husband's doing that brings the future lovers together. Judging from other works (e.g., *Guillaume au faucon*) that use similar methods, audiences clearly took considerable pleasure in seeing husbands

---

[8] The suspension of disbelief is a prerequisite for the perception of humor in most fabliaux, as in jokes and certain other comic forms. These are works that confer remarkable power on the narrators, who are exempted from the usual constraints of reality and realism alike.

unwittingly concoct their own cuckolding. The husband's unconscious complicity constitutes the primary appeal of the poem.

Guillaume au faucon shares more than a single characteristic with this fabliau. In that work, the conclusion is reached in a very similar way: Guillaume is fasting in protest of his lady's refusal to return his love. She rebukes him for his temerity and eventually threatens to inform her husband of his advances. Upon the husband's return, she repeatedly offers Guillaume one last chance to give up his foolhardy fast, going so far as to reveal to her husband that Guillaume had come into her chamber and made an improper request. Again, she twice offers Guillaume a way out: "I am going to tell my husband what you said; will you eat now?" (39-42, 51-53). The young man responds that he will never take food and drink until the pain that is in his heart is soothed (558-59).

At that point occurs the pivot that prepares the solution to the dilemma. The lady's threats have clearly become tests, and Guillaume has passed them all by demonstrating his willingness to die for love of her, either from fasting or from her husband's sword. That pivot is signaled by the key line (560), "Lors en ot la dame pitié" ("Then the lady took pity on him"). She tells her husband that Guillaume has asked for one of his falcons (the "faucon" of the text constituting a sly pun—"two words in one," says the author, and two rewards in one, the word being the homophone of "faux con" ("false or substitute cunt"; see 607-14) and that she had no right to give away what was his. The husband immediately offers it, and the woman notes—another *double-entendre*, 563-66—that "if my husband has given it to you, I have no right to withhold it."

The young man's purpose is not unlike that of the knight in *Du chevalier qui recovra l'amor de sa dame*, and when another request is substituted for his, it is the woman's husband who insists that it be granted, thus contributing to his own cuckolding. These two works, in no way analogues in terms of motifs, are strikingly similar in regard to the mechanism of the intrigue. The primary distinction between them is that we are explicitly told that the wife in *Guillaume au faucon* took pity on him (560) and, when he later enters the room, that Love, or Cupid, had shot his arrow at her (589).

Again, the question of "courtly" fabliaux arises. I identified in *Du chevalier qui recovra l'amor de sa dame* a pivot, a point at which a text that had all the marks of a lai or a seriously courtly story turned perceptibly into a fabliaux. That point, of course, begs the question of generic definition treated in my second chapter, since I implied that the distinction between a fabliaux and other kinds of short narratives was by no means sharp. Nonetheless, to the extent that we can identify such a pivot, shifting the work from a serious courtly tale to an amusing anecdote, we have defined one characteristic of at least certain fabliaux.

In *Guillaume au faucon*, we find not only such a pivot, in the narratorial comment to the effect that the woman took pity on Guillaume, but also an earlier thematic discrepancy that ought to have alerted the reader to the probability that something was awry in this tale of long-suffering courtly love. I refer not only to the fact that it is a squire, not a knight, who pines for love of the lady, but also that, in one important way, the lady does not correspond to our expectations regarding a courtly lady. Her beauty is incomparable, it is true, and the narrator exercises his rhetorical gifts to describe it in great detail. Traditionally, a lady could be and often was haughty and disdainful, particularly when one apparently unworthy of her sought her love. This woman, however, is simply of poor character; she is "mal aprise" (30), and she is typical of fabliaux women who, once they know they are loved, will go to any lengths to torture the lover. It may be going too far to suggest that such a generalization about women could not occur in a "courtly tale" (although there, too, it ought to serve as a signal to the reader that something atypical or untoward will happen), but it is far more typical of the texts we customarily identify as fabliaux.

*

Du chevalier qui recovra l'amor de sa dame and, perhaps, *Guillaume au faucon* may be unexpected choices of texts with which to begin a chapter devoted at least in part to the courtliness of the fabliau. Most readers familiar with fabliau criticism would expect instead any one of a group of fabliaux that give evidence of courtly "parody," and indeed that is a subject that bears discussion. Yet, whatever our conclusion about parodic intent in some fabliaux, it is important to note that, as *Du chevalier qui recovra l'amor de sa dame* indicates, we have some fabliaux that are indeed courtly, in terms of their context, their language, and the social level of the characters, but that give no evidence of the kind of parody that Per Nykrog identified in many representatives of the corpus.[9]

Nykrog began his corresponding chapter (III) with a discussion of *Aloul*, and there are certainly a good many other texts that provide striking examples of what Nykrog (p. 74) calls "la courtoisie du vilain." *Aloul* tells a rollicking story of a priest who effortlessly seduces a woman, later climbs in bed with her husband, and soon has to fight fiercely to retain possession of his testicles. But the imagery that introduces this story speaks of May, nightingales, the sweetness of a dewy morning in a grove, and love; and, after satisfying his lust, the priest announces that he is the woman's *amis* and *drus* (106).

Nykrog goes on to mention a number of typically courtly images and formulas drawn from other fabliaux (see p. 74). It will suffice to refer again to a single example, discussed in chapter I and also by Nykrog: *Cele qui se fist foutre sur la fosse de son mari*. In that work, the squire, having wagered that he can seduce a widow, informs her that he has already killed his lady, "qui mout estoit cortoise et sage" ("who was very courtly and wise," 85), and when asked how he did it, he replies "en fotant" (88). The comic shock value of "en fotant" is amplified by its juxtaposition with the preceding courtly formula.

As this example and others indicate, the authors of fabliaux did not lack familiarity with a more elevated vocabulary and diction, and a good many of them make use of courtly language for comic or other purposes. Some of the texts in question, like *Guillaume au faucon*, develop within a largely refined context.[10] But courtly language may also occur in decidedly "uncourtly" fabliaux, such as *Les Quatre Sohais Saint Martin*. As I discuss this text in more detail elsewhere, it will suffice to note here that the wife (who "wears the pants" in the family, 35) thinks little of her husband and addresses him abusively ("Vilains, mal jor aies!," "Peasant, may you have a bad day," 36) until the day he tells her that St. Martin granted him four wishes that can make him a wealthy man. She immediately responds, in

---

[9] See esp. pp. 72-93.

[10] However, *Cele qui se fist foutre sur la fosse de son mari* is situated somewhere between courtly and *vilain*, not only because one character is a knight, but because squires were themselves so situated: their origin may have been noble, but their duties cast them in the role of servants.

impeccable courtly diction, ". . . biaus dolz amis, / Je ai en vos tot mon cuer mis!" ("my fair sweet friend, I have given you all my love," 61-62). In addition, she abandons the familiar form of address, *tu*, in favor of *vos*, *vous*, to express her newfound respect for him.[11] Courtliness is thus to be found in texts where it would not be expected, and expressed by uncultivated and even base characters.

Nykrog's thesis, revolutionary when published in 1957, was eventually embraced by most scholars and became a commonplace of fabliau criticism. Recently, however, we have seen some reaction against his views. Ménard, for example, refutes Nykrog and concludes that ". . . on est bien forcé de constater que la parodie est absente, ou du moins exceptionnelle, dans les fabliaux" (p. 210).

Ménard's contention merits consideration. Throughout his book, he attempts to correct generalizations and imprecise terminology, insisting, for example, that American scholars have been careless in failing to draw a distinction between "comedy" and "humor," pp. 223-24. In my view, he is correct to look skeptically at *any* critical notion so unquestioningly accepted as that of fabliau parody, although the primary culprits here may well be critics since Nykrog, and not Nykrog himself.

But Ménard also goes farther, insisting that parody is an "art de référence," according to which a later text alludes specifically to an earlier one (pp. 207-08); and he accuses those who speak about fabliau parody of not taking the trouble to support their contention with specific proof of imitation. He suggests that we can cite few or no examples of particular texts that are parodied in the fabliaux. Here again, I approve of his insistence on methodological rigor; but I would take exception to the narrowness of his definition of parody, if for no other reason than that we lack a term to identify "a direct parodic borrowing from a courtly situation" or diction.[12]

In any case, Ménard's conclusions will only cloud the issue if their result, or their purpose, is to make us neglect the phenomenon that

---

[11] A far more extended discussion of this fabliau is offered by E. Jane Burns in the first chapter of *Bodytalk: When Women Speak in Old French Literature* (Philadelphia: University of Pennsylvania Press, 1993).

[12] Richard O'Gorman, ed., *Les Braies au Cordelier* (Birmingham: Summa, 1983), p. 13.

we have identified—even if inaccurately—as parody. Ménard does not, in fact, deny that the language used in *Aloul* and many another text is characteristic of courtly romance; he suggests instead that they occur as the result of an author's attempt to create "effets de dissonance" (p. 212).

Certainly we cannot doubt that an audience, hearing of a priest concluding a sudden sexual attack on a woman by announcing that he is her *amis* and *drus*, would appreciate the disparity, the dissonance, between deed and word; nor would that audience fail to recognize the context from which the language is drawn, and that context is indisputably courtly. Perhaps the author is not parodying a specific text, but he is just as clearly using language spoken routinely by characters in courtly romance.

Ménard's reference to dissonance is well taken here. The contrast of stylistic levels or the contrast between animal lust and courtly diction provides the essential comedy of the scene. Similarly, in *Cele qui se fist foutre sur la fosse de son mari*, a part of the humor derives from the juxtaposition of the squire's description of his lady as "cortoise et sage" with his immediate confession that he killed her "en fotant"; and it is also significant that the words he has spoken to the lady until that point are courtly but that he, a squire, is not—a further dissonance.

Courtly diction so permeated the thirteenth-century literary world that we can easily suppose certain uses of courtly language to have been almost unconscious. What, for example, are we to make of the first two lines of *La Borgoise d'Orliens*, which promise us a very courtly story about a bourgeois woman ("d'une bourjoise une aventure asés courtoise")? Perhaps "aventure courtoise" can be, in some instances, little more than a conventional designation for a "pleasing story." If we see it as a small but significant dissonance, however, the ironic effect of the term *courtoise* becomes apparent as we read farther and find the story of a woman who entertains her lover even as her husband is being beaten by the servants (and is enjoying it, since the woman has arranged matters so that he believes the beating to be proof of her fidelity).

We should surely not go as far as Ménard in suggesting (p. 209) that the priest in *Aloul* speaks as he does because there is no other way to speak when making a declaration of love, but we can at least conceive of situations in which we need ascribe no particular intent to such diction. On the other hand, if we cannot in every instance determine, in regard to a particular text, the intent of diction we would describe as courtly, we can be certain that, on balance, authors who use it in apparently inappropriate contexts do so for a well-defined purpose. An inventory of the situations in which humor arises from a contrast between courtly and uncourtly styles or situations would provide, I believe, persuasive evidence of the intentional and systematic borrowing of courtly formulas for comic purposes. The term "parody" may be both unnecessary and misleading, but what we have identified by that name is not only real but an essential element in the successful elaboration of many fabliaux.

Thus, in regard to the courtliness of fabliaux, we have, not surprisingly, a gamut or continuum. First, the very idea of courtliness when we are reading certain fabliaux would strike us as ludicrous. In other works, we could identify phrases or sentiments that occur frequently in courtly tales but that the author may have used, without specific intent, simply because they were familiar and ready-made expressions, a stock part of his lexical repertoire. The group of texts that has attracted the most attention includes *Aloul* and *Cele qui se fist foutre*, in which, for comic purposes, authors make apparently calculated use of courtly language drawn from courtly literary contexts (though not necessarily from a particular text) and in which the effectiveness of the comedy depends on the audience's perception of that appropriation. Finally—and this takes us back to the beginning of this chapter—we have works in which the courtliness is neither an incidental feature of the text nor a borrowing intended to provoke laughter by its juxtaposition with uncourtly elements: they are texts whose *courtoisie* is not a *courtoisie du vilain*. In these works, the context and characters are authentically courtly,[13] but that courtliness is the more remarkable and more effective because it is in no way incompatible with the humorous elaboration of an anecdote.

---

[13] As Nykrog notes (p. 74), in regard to *Chevalier qui recovra l'amor de sa dame*, the *Lai d'Aristote*, and *Auberee*, "tout, langage, sentiments, actions, est presque strictement conforme aux exigences courtoises . . . ."

V. Women in the Fabliaux

Text: *De la dame escolliee*

618 lines
MR, VI, 95-116

[A woman contradicts her husband in everything, so when a young count (who has fallen in love with their daughter because of her reputed beauty, but without seeing her) comes to their home, the husband refuses him hospitality, thereby ensuring that his wife will disagree and welcome the young man. The husband further suggests concealing his daughter from the young man, only to have his wife contradict him and introduce the young people to each other. The couple marry, and when the young woman, following her mother's suggestions, once countermands her husband's orders, he beats her nearly to death, effectively correcting her behavior. Her parents come to visit, and the count announces to his mother-in-law that her outrageous pride is due to her having testicles. He has her restrained and slices her thighs, palming bull testicles he had earlier sent for. Expressing fear that they may grow back, he prepares to cauterize the wound; the terrified woman swears that she is cured and promises never again to contradict her husband. The count threatens his wife with similar treatment if she is not perpetually submissive and obedient.]

De la dame escolliee, in which a condemnation of women is premise as well as conclusion, has achieved some notoriety as one of the most misogynistic texts belonging to a misogynistic genre. In terms of its treatment of its female characters, most readers will find little to commend it. But before we condemn it, however justifiably, for its narrator's practice of savoring an unsavory subject, we should at least examine the work systematically to determine whether it has redeeming literary value. In fact, we will find that this composition is far more than an unadorned attack on women, although it is undeniably that as well. It is more narratively effective than some readers may have recognized, and its construction deserves not to be ignored in favor of its theme. It is also significant for its narrative complexity, for it provides three separate but thoroughly interrelated sequences, any one of which could stand alone. Whether it is also funny or not depends, obviously, on individual tastes.

The poem begins with an address to *Seignor* ("Lords"), addressing its message specifically to males, rather than to the traditional generalized audience. More particularly, the reference is to married men who give their wives authority over them and therefore bring shame on themselves. The narrator proposes to offer "une essanple petite" (a "small lesson," 5), and whereas similar formulas are sometimes used as a conveniently vague label for a fabliau, it appears in this case to be instead a very specific reference to the intent of this text, a story with a rigorous though, for most readers, misguided "moral" message. (The narrator does identify the text as a fabliau, but only in the conclusion, 617.)

Having announced a story, the author might be expected to begin. Instead, he elaborates on his purpose, noting, with a logic that we may find curious but that nonetheless operates consistently within this story, that women who are treated too well by their husbands love them less for it. He goes on to urge men to punish foolish women ("les foles," 11), thereby teaching them proper love and obedience. He concludes his introduction with a warning: women who behave improperly will pay for it ("ce est lor honte," 17).

Or rather, I should say that the narrator *appeared* to conclude with line 17, for he then launches, a third time, into the same warning, concerning the dishonor that comes to men who make their wives their lords. We find ourselves at line 25 before the anecdote begins.[1] The vehemence and insistence of the author must impress us, whatever may be our view of his misogyny; and the several returns to the moral of the story (announced before the story begins) serve to dispel any suspicion we may have had that the author was indulging in irony when he suggested that kindness to women is invariably met by a waning of love. There is no reason to assume, in the first twenty-four lines, that the author is not entirely serious or that he does not mean to be taken literally; and if that is so, we must already suspect

---

[1] However, the particular details of this introduction vary from manuscript to manuscript; I discuss it further in Chapter VII.

that we are about to encounter one of the most misogynistic of fabliaux. We will not be disappointed.

At every turn, the author joins his thesis to the exposition of his anecdote. For example, it will not suffice for him to note simply that the wife is overbearing or that her husband is henpecked. Instead, he offers us an explanation (she hates him), and he moreover gives us the reason for her hatred (28-32): he loved her so much that he gave her everything, from possessions to authority. The unsubtle implication is that this is no way to treat a woman; indeed, it stretches a point to call it an implication, for the author tells us quite directly that he loved and gave her everything, *wherefore* (*Dont*, 33) she held him in contempt.

While we should be cautious about drawing conclusions from sentiments expressed within a fictional text, and especially a fabliau, those expressed here sound very much like an unmediated intrusion of authorial opinion. That intrusion produces two results: readers are likely to find in this work an unadorned hatred of women and to attribute that view to the author; and this narrator is far more individualized than those of most fabliaux. While we may disapprove of what he says, we remain aware of his presence; he is far more "real" than the conventionalized "I" or "je" of many other texts. On the other hand, the specificity of the narrator's presence contrasts with the vagueness of the characters; they are scarcely developed at all, and they tend to be presented with fewer nuances even than most fabliau characters. Emphasis remains entirely on the action, as these characters serve as little more than symbolic representations of certain qualities; we have here not a human drama, but an almost abstract battle of the sexes, the story of a Corrupt Woman Properly Chastened.

Following the exposition of the wife's domineering ways, we learn of the couple's beautiful daughter (37ff.) and of a count who, based on reports of her beauty, had come to love her without having seen her. He very much wants to meet her (52). Now, coincidences occur in fabliaux,[2] and they generally do not require explanation: the count is hunting when it begins to rain, and it happens that the man near whose home he takes shelter is her father, our henpecked husband. When the man explains that his wife contradicts him at every turn,

---

[2] For a discussion of (apparent) coincidences, see Chapter X.

the count laughs and notes, in what this poem presents as the voice of reason, that if the husband had been valiant (*preuz*, 104), he would not have permitted such a situation to develop.

The husband may be submissive, but at least he knows how to get his way, for he knows that his wife will contradict his every wish and statement. Thus, by refusing to welcome the count, to feed him, and to introduce him to his daughter, he ensures that his wife will offer the young man a warm welcome, a sumptuous feast, and the company of their daughter. In regard to the last, the author even tells us (157) that the mother did not want the young woman to be seen, but she immediately changes her mind when her husband urges her to have their daughter dine in another room: all her other desires and preferences, indeed her better judgment, pale before her need to contradict her husband.

Having won the young woman's hand, the count refuses to accept a dowry; the author intrudes to approve that decision, remarking that the man who has a good woman has much. But the narratorial bias of this text is such that he finds it necessary to insist on the converse as well: he who takes a bad wife has nothing (222).

The story might have closed here: the husband has craftily deceived his shrewish wife and, through manipulation, has gained what he sought. The woman, caught in the trap of her own contrary ways, grants to the count what he, too, was seeking. We have perhaps smiled both at the husband's cleverness and at the wife's willingness to ignore her own wishes in order to frustrate his, and the young couple are quickly married. We have here a complete and self-contained story, the integrity of which is troubled only by the author's indication (in the prologue and elsewhere) that we are not to admire the husband. The disparity between authorial views and the narratively satisfactory conclusion—that is, the fact that the husband can be at the same time successful and entirely undeserving of approbation—is sufficient to prevent a full closure here, and the story clearly must continue.

Thus comes the time for the parents to offer advice to the young bride, and this scene (223ff.) provides the link between the first and second divisions of the work; it is an extraordinary scene that merits attention and has generally received it from readers. Yet, in fact, most of the attention it has had is focused on the mother's advice, as she admonishes the bride to treat her own husband the way she (the mother) has treated hers: the daughter is to put herself above her husband, ignore his will, and contradict his every word and desire. Only in that way, we are told, can she have *honor* (237); that is a statement that clearly does not reflect the view of a narrator who earlier referred to the *honte* of domineering women (17) and the *deshenor* (22) of men who tolerate such behavior.

The mother's statement contradicts not only those narratorial views, but also the words of the father, who will tell her (224, 226; repeated 250-52)[3] that *honeur* will come to her if she respects her husband, *honte* if she does not. The woman's remarkable speech, by its exaggeration and lack of nuance, as well as by its direct contradiction of the narrator's and husband's views, leaves little doubt concerning the opinion the poet would have us accept. Indeed, although we may have some difficulty accepting it without question, such an attitude would permit us to see that subsequent events are natural, logical, and even necessary.

Readers often overlook the role of the woman's father in this passage; yet his advice preceded that of his wife and was repeated after she spoke. Prior to her harangue, he had, as I noted, counseled his daughter to respect her husband. Perhaps we cannot legitimately speculate on his motivation; it is after all unusual for fabliau characters to have any motivation that the author does not clearly explain. Perhaps the man simply wanted to offer sound advice. Nonetheless, he certainly knew that his wife would contradict whatever advice he gave, and indeed she does. He thus provokes her diatribe, which eventually causes the young woman to contradict her husband, an act that in turns leads to her punishment and eventual transformation into an "ideal wife." Whatever the husband's intent, his words serve as a catalyst for the remainder of the story, and, having forever lost his own honor, he is at least instrumental in assuring his daughter's. He even provides the tools of his daughter's lesson, by giving the count two greyhounds and a palfrey.

That this is a battle of the sexes, with the ultimate victor preordained, is indicated by the count's wondering, before there is any apparent need for it, how he might properly train his wife and

---

[3] In this text, views that apparently echo the author's are emphasized by repetition: the prologue repeats its sentiments three times; the father repeats his twice.

ensure that she will be unlike her mother; his obvious assumption is: "like mother, like daughter." That he is scarcely too suspicious was indicated by the young woman's assurance to her mother that she would, if possible, follow her advice; she had not responded to her father's counsel. The count finds the pretext he needs when the two dogs disobey him by failing to catch a hare and when the horse (who in fact does not hear the command: "ne l'entendi," 286) then disobeys his order not to graze: the man beheads them all, thereafter explaining to his bride that he killed them because they disobeyed him.[4]

Apparently, it does not suffice to observe lessons, however brutal; the woman has to experience one herself, and when she contradicts her husband once, merely by telling the cook to prepare only garlic sauces, rather than the varied sauces ordered by the count, the outraged husband ignores her protestations that she has repented and has learned her lesson. He first punishes the cook, putting out his eye, cutting off an ear and a hand, and exiling him; if we can assume that this punishment fits the crime, then we must conclude that the husband considers obedience to a woman to be a grievous offense. Then he clubs his wife into unconsciousness, injuring her so severely that her recuperation requires three months. The narrator tells us however that she recovers as a result of the count's excellent care. We are *not* told that she never again presumes to disobey him, but that, apparently, goes without saying. Similarly implicit in the fabliau is the threat of renewed violence, should it be required in response to renewed presumptuousness.

Perhaps surprisingly, the count, while severely berating his wife and telling her that she cannot be pardoned without punishment, nonetheless addresses her as "dame" (369), "douce amie" (374), and "bele" (383); that is, "lady," "dear friend," and "beautiful one." He never calls her, as some fabliau characters might, a fool or a slut. What are we to make of his polite and (especially with "douce amie") courtly diction? Could it be sarcasm or mock politeness? Or might it

---

[4] This portion of the work has a close, and just slightly less brutal, analogue in a modern joke concerning a newlywed couple. As they leave the church in a buggy, the horse stumbles, and the man calls out "That's one!" Soon the horse stumbles a second time, and he says "That's two!" When it happens again, he says "That's three!" and shoots the horse. The woman begins to berate her husband; he waits until she pauses and then says, quietly, "That's one."

be that the author is simply using stock formulas of address, with no particular intent? On the contrary, there appears to be no reason not to assume that he means precisely what he says, particularly when he is meticulously attentive to his wife's medical needs. That he takes the best of care of her until she is healed suggests that, at least in his own way, he genuinely loves her. If that is so, we must also conclude that the beating was similarly motivated by love, and if that is a conception of love that we find difficult to accept, it is nevertheless a perfectly simple and consistent expression of the conservative spirit I traced in an earlier chapter.

Obviously, when she is behaving "properly," she reestablishes a social and sexual equilibrium that permits him to treat her with deference and respect. That is, a literal interpretation of his words reinforces the overt "lesson" of this text: the natural order of things has man as the master of woman; if she inverts that natural order, it is the duty of the male to reestablish it. And not only is it right, but it is for the benefit of all concerned: the count is beating his wife for her own good as well as for his own benefit, for the sake of the marriage, and, presumably, for the edification of all who hear this *essanple*.

If the first division of the fabliau was left at least partially open, thereby occasioning the poem's continuation, the closure at this point is more complete: the young woman has transgressed her authority, she has been chastened for her presumption, and she has apparently learned her lesson. But we are not finished yet. First, our author is not one to abandon this kind of subject without milking it thoroughly. And second, there is one loose end, the kind that would doubtless disturb him: the mother is still practicing her tyranny on her husband. Such a habit requires correction and retribution, and the author and count are just the people to provide them. Thus, line 395 announces, as if beginning a new tale, "D'un autre essanple oez la somme" ("Now listen to the meaning of another exemplum").

The third part unites the two couples again and provides retribution for the mother, depicts the father's release from his subservience, and offers a stern and effective warning for the count's wife. In other words, it ties up all the loose ends. It is in the final section that physical cruelty and overt misogyny come most to the fore. We should, however, note the thematic and narrative symmetry between the second and third sections of the story: a woman who is disobedient is punished physically and threatened (once implicitly, once explicitly) with further punishment; she reforms. And in this text's version of poetic justice, the pain inflicted on the mother is, if not more serious, at least more striking and described in more lavish detail than that endured by the daughter. The results are similar, too: she survives and eventually recovers, owing to the care provided by her husband and a good physician, and she is cured, always loving and obeying her husband thereafter.

That the count is twice enforcing what he considers the natural order of things is indicated by the nature of the stratagem he uses to punish the older woman. He announces that she has testicles and that they must be removed. That is, she is not simply a woman who misbehaves; she is a woman who is specifically emulating the behavior of a man. We have more than one expression in colloquial English to describe such behavior, indicating that we have perhaps inherited the count's views: an acceptable expression refers to "wearing the pants in the family," whereas a less acceptable one corresponds very closely to the count's accusation against the woman.

The narratorial commentary resumes at the end, as the author tells us (608-09) that the count had acted admirably, and he adds "Bless him." The concluding moral of the story is "Dahet feme qui despit home!" ("Cursed be the woman who hates men," 618), a precept likely to appear odd to those who see in this work less hatred of men by women than hatred of women by the narrator. In his defense, one might point out that the author does not condemn women in general, but rather *males femes* (610), defined as those who spite or hate men. Yet his reference to women who are *bones* (613) carries no great conviction, perhaps because, for the count if not for the narrator himself, one assumes and expects the worst.

Unless we happen to share the narrator's misogyny, we are not likely to find this fabliau very funny or even very pleasant. I confess that I do not; this text provides a severe test of scholarly detachment. Nonetheless, the fact that we may find the subject thoroughly repugnant should not prevent us from reading the work in its own terms and appreciating the construction of the tale: it is somewhat more intricate than many fabliaux, it is well balanced, structurally if not psychologically, and certain narrative subtleties in the work replace the thematic subtleties that are scarcely in evidence.

It is a tripartite text, with the second and third sections flowing logically out of the preceding one, with the middle part itself divided into three parts (killing of the dogs, killing of the horse, beating of the wife), and with the final sequence tying up all the loose ends: it punishes and corrects the older woman, reinforces the lesson given to the younger one, liberates the father from his wife's tyranny, confirms the count's sovereignty, and in general reestablishes the "proper" relationship between men and women.

Yet, however much we may praise the poem's structure and its narrative effectiveness, the fabliau has most often attracted attention for its unadorned misogyny. But the fact that its repugnant theme may disguise its compositional skill is precisely the reason I chose it as the text to open a discussion of women in the fabliaux. There can be no significant doubt about the misogyny of this work, but, as we shall see, it is not always so easy to draw conclusions about fabliau views of women. We must therefore look closely at several quite dissimilar compositions in order to draw even the most tentative of conclusions.

*

The traditional assessment of fabliau attitudes toward women requires no lengthy rehearsal here.[5] Until recent years, readers and critics simply took for granted the fundamental misogyny of fabliaux. However, a revisionist spirit has led several recent scholars to challenge this traditional assumption, either denying the misogynistic intent of authors altogether or, with Lorcin, contending that the fabliaux, while perhaps antifeminist, were no more so than other medieval genres.[6] Philippe Ménard, for example, insists that it would

---

[5] Nor, for that matter, does the broader subject of medieval misogyny require rehearsal. Readers who seek information on that subject, whether in the writings of the church fathers, in law, or in everyday life, will find it in abundance. The subject has recently been treated by R. Howard Bloch in *Medieval Misogyny and the Invention of Western Romantic Love* (Chicago: University of Chicago Press, 1991).

[6] Marie-Thérèse Lorcin, *Façons de sentir et de penser: les fabliaux français* (Paris: Champion, 1979), p. 174. See also Muscatine, p. 122: ". . . the so-called 'antifeminism' in the fabliaux is so various in its quality and tone as more often to support the claim of admiration for women than fear and hatred."

be entirely wrong ("tout à fait erroné") to believe that fabliau authors harbored malevolent views of women, and he concludes that fabliau antifeminism "n'est qu'une petite façade et reste très limité."[7]

Clearly, the difficulty with both the traditional view and the one espoused by Ménard is that they consist of wholesale generalizations, not always based on the study of particular texts. Furthermore, they are in certain cases generalizations flatly stated and intended to be taken as self-evident and not open to question; for example, Lorcin (p. 174) suggests in fact that her conclusion is so obvious that there is simply no point in examining the problem further.

That opinion notwithstanding, I think a reconsideration may prove to be profitable. It will certainly support the view that (to borrow Raymond Eichmann's delightful understatement) "some fabliaux are not favorable to women."[8] More important still, it will demonstrate clearly—and this is a crucial corrective to traditional assessments—that we simply cannot make generalizations applicable to the fabliaux uniformly, whether about the treatment of women or about any other theme or subject; as I have emphasized more than once, we are, after all, dealing with a great many texts composed during a century and a half. Curiously, while we readily accept the essential variety of other genres, we continue to make categorical statements about the fabliaux, as though they somehow follow a strict formula or, at least, ought to do so. If we are ever to appreciate and understand the genre fully, we shall have to begin by respecting its richness and essential diversity. As a preliminary step, we must acknowledge that the fabliaux present various views, not *a view*, of women. Some of them, such as *La Borgoise d'Orliens* and *Berengier au lonc cul*, either praise her explicitly or show her happily triumphant over a husband who

---

[7] *Les Fabliaux*, p. 138. I would concur with his judgment, were we dealing only with a certain number of the fabliaux. It is hard not to dissent, however, after reading such texts as *De la dame escolliee*.

[8] See his "The Antifeminism of the Fabliaux," in *Authors and Philosophers* (Columbia: University of South Carolina Press, 1979), p. 27. Compare, however, E. Jane Burns's remark, in *Bodytalk: When Women Speak in Old French Literature* (Philadelphia: University of Pennsylvania Press, 1993), that "[a]lthough most of the 150 fabliaux . . . are not essentially about women, the genre as a whole bears the marks of misogynous comedy" (p. 27).

may be a weakling or a coward[9]; others indisputably revile her. In a few she is presented with a gentle humor or irony, while some texts, including the one analyzed above, propose that nothing less than physical violence be used to keep a woman in her place.

We cannot therefore be satisfied with the simple statement: "fabliau authors are misogynists." But the question is more complicated yet: it will not suffice to identify either a mistreated or a scheming woman in order to corroborate the charge of misogyny, nor to find a virtuous woman in order to refute that charge. We must go beyond a simple description of a woman's actions and role in a fabliau and must consider authorial point of view and presentation as well. Even then, we encounter perplexing difficulties. For example, if a woman is praised for her scheming and craftiness, may we take that as an approbative view of woman, since she *is* at least praised? Or should we conclude instead that the text is antifeminist, since the author is praising her for less than admirable qualities?[10] In fact, neither is justified without a close examination of the particular text; unless we take into account the context and the narratorial attitude, we risk saying more about ourselves than about the texts.

The two characteristics most often attributed to fabliau women are deceitfulness and cupidity, and it goes without saying that the two are often allied in a single text. Even a woman's protestations of indifference to sex are unable to conceal for long her insatiable appetites. *Auberee* is revealing in this regard. After conspiring to unite the young man with the married woman whom he loves but who wants nothing to do with him, Auberee advises him to ignore the woman if she screams, to join her in bed and then all will go well. The man follows directions and even adds a bit of blackmail by asking what others, attracted by screams, would say if they found the

---

[9] Although this statement is often true—the husband of women who are praiseworthy are often old, stupid, or cruel—I am not persuaded that it is essential to diminish the man in order to praise the woman or let her triumph.

[10] Or may we perhaps take it that in the absence of an explicit moral about women, the narrator's view, whatever it may be, is applicable only to this particular character? That is, however, an extreme position; it assumes no link between literary texts and the society and attitudes that produced them. This position is, to my mind, no more defensible than the opposite (and similarly extreme) notion: that a text necessarily provides an accurate reflection of an author's attitudes.

two of them together in bed. Then, we learn, she forgets her "pride" (a curious way to refer to a married woman's refusal to commit adultery!) and does "what they were there to do."

Examples abound. In *Porcelet* and *La Dame qui aveine demandoit pour Morel sa provende avoir*, the woman's desires are so insatiable that she exhausts her poor husband. In *Le Fevre de Creil*, the woman finds the mere curiosity about the apprentice's organ irresistible.[11] In *Le Prestre qui abevete*, the priest lifts the woman's dress and satisfies the desires of both of them, but the narrator describes it as "doing that thing that women love most" (57-58), ignoring the abundant evidence that fabliau priests seem scarcely less devoted to sexual pleasure than, as this narrator insists, are women. In the last example, it was the priest, not the woman, who took the initiative. Were we to judge their actions objectively, they would both be guilty, but he even more than she because he conceived and executed the plan that united them. Yet the narratorial intervention emphasizes *her* desires, constituting a criticism of her and reminding us of the pervasiveness of a certain male notion that, secretly, all women "want it."

This example suggests that if we are seriously to evaluate fabliau views of women, it may be productive to consider commentary more than simple content. In passing quickly over the anecdotal content of the works, I am by no means suggesting that antifeminist sentiments are not to be found there; they are indeed present and are perhaps more insidious when implied by narrative development than when stated explicitly. I have chosen, however, to concentrate on commentary more than content for two reasons. First, the anecdote itself may be drawn from stories, taken from other times or places, that provide the narrative detail, but the commentary is ordinarily the fabliau author's own. Second, judgments regarding misogynistic content of a work are more open to subjective interpretation and to dispute. For present purposes, therefore, I will draw no conclusions from unflattering portraits of women or from the assumption, which is nonetheless significant, that in many fabliaux women are seen as object or receptacle, whose purpose is simply to provide service or

---

[11] More precisely, as R. Howard Bloch correctly notes in *The Scandal of the Fabliaux* (Chicago: University of Chicago Press, 1986), p. 91, it is her husband's description that excites her interest; the appeal is more linguistic than anatomical.

gratification to a man. Nor will I go beyond *De la dame escolliee* in identifying cruel and unusual treatment to which a woman may be subjected; after all, it is sometimes the husband who is beaten or mistreated, as, for example, in *La Borgoise d'Orliens*, and if the two cases are different, it is not because of the narrative facts, but rather because of point of view, presentation, and commentary.

As critics have sometimes noted, male as well as female characters are subject to censure in the fabliaux. We do not have to look far to find men who are presented as loutish, cruel, or naive. But there is one crucial difference between the presentation of men and women: when men are criticized, it is because they are less than admirable individuals; when women are criticized, even for the same failings, they are most often presented as representatives of their sex. In the fabliaux, generalizations about a sex always concern women. This is true even in works that engage our sympathies on the side of the female character. For example, *La Borgoise d'Orliens* presents a woman whose resourcefulness we are likely to find more admirable than reprehensible. Yet the author cannot resist taking her as a typical example of her sex; he notes that she wants to catch her husband in his own trap, but while the husband is apparently blameless in trying to entrap her, she is a characteristically devious female: "Eles [women in general] ont meint homes dechu" ("They have deceived many a man," 118).

The general situation described here is in evidence in a good many works. That is, there are relatively few genuinely admirable characters of either sex in the fabliaux.[12] As I have suggested, the deceitfulness of the woman is often matched by the loutishness of the man, and his stupidity may surpass her cupidity. Under those circumstances, the author often has a reasonable choice between two morals, and we can take it as a nearly invariable axiom of the genre that when that is the case, he will choose the one most critical of women. Thus, while the author of *Cele qui se fist foutre sur la fosse de son mari* describes certain men as fools, he explains his justification in predictable fashion:

---

[12] One of the exceptions is the *vilain* of the *Vilain qui conquist paradis par plait*.

Por ce tain je celui a fol
Qui trop met en fame sa cure.
Que trop est de foible nature:
De noiant rit, de noiant plore,
Fame aime et het en petit d'ore;
Tost li est talans remeüz.
Qui fame croit s'est deceüz.

("For this reason I consider him a fool who puts his trust in a woman; for women are weak: they laugh for no reason, weep for no reason. Women love and hate lightly; their desires quickly change. Whoever believes a woman is a fool," 108-14)

A somewhat similar conclusion is offered by *Le Vilain de Bailleul*, in which a woman convinces her husband that he is dead; being "dead," he is powerless to interfere when he witnesses a passionate encounter between her and the priest. Although the husband has been described as hideous and ugly, and although his stupidity is unsurpassed in the fabliaux, the author manages to turn the moral against women as much as against him: ". . . on doit por fol tenir celui / Qui mieus croit sa fame que lui" ("He who believes his wife rather than himself should be considered a fool," 115-16). The two fabliaux just cited offer more a qualification than a contradiction of my suggestion that men remain individuals while women become types. The morals of the stories do offer general observations about *some* men—but specifically they are men foolish enough to be taken in *by women*.

An interesting development of the moral is offered by *La Bourse pleine de Sens*. A man who has both a wife and a mistress tests them both and learns that his wife loves him truly and deeply, while the mistress is interested only in his possessions. The lesson to be drawn from this experience concerns mistresses: "fous est qui y tient aliance" ("he is a fool who keeps company with them," 414); since there is no love or fidelity in them, it is foolish to be faithful to them or to give them anything. In the context of the poem, this moral is appropriate but incomplete, because the author virtually ignores the wife, who is the model of fidelity and unselfishness, willing to sell everything she owns when she thinks her husband has lost his wealth. The author does indeed add a second moral, noting that "encor a ou

fablel du sen" ("there is yet another moral in this fabliau," 416).
When he notes that the man who has a good wife is foolish to seek
out a *garce*, we may anticipate praise of that "good wife," but instead
we learn that "Ausi est cuer de fame ouvert / Tot tens por home
decevoir" ("A women's heart is always ready to deceive a man," 420-
21).

Finally, we should note that after the brutal mutilation that occurs
in *De la dame escolliee*, the moral makes no mention of this torture.
On the contrary, the work implies that the mutilation was a necessary
and quite justified corrective to her behavior, concluding, as noted
earlier, by the warning: "Dahet feme qui despit home" ("Cursed be
the woman who disdains men," 618).

The most reliable indication of textual attitudes, whether about
women or about anything else, is often given by works that do not
ostensibly concern that subject. Most often, we will find that the views
of women I have identified above will prevail throughout the fabliaux.
A telling example is provided by *La Crote*.[13] Although its
protagonists are husband and wife, the text does not deal with strife
between them, with infidelity, or even, at least directly, with
sovereignty. We run a risk if we insist on finding a lesson in every
fabliau. In *La Crote*, the author appears to have been less concerned
with the exemplary value of the anecdote than with its crudely
humorous possibilities, but that is precisely the point: the author's
assumptions about masculine and feminine roles is revealed even in
the absence of any apparent intent to treat that subject. In fact, this
narrative deals with the reestablishment of what fabliau narrators
routinely consider the "appropriate" relationship of wife to husband.
The events chasten the woman, as many fabliaux do, for she vows
never again to wager with her husband. Indeed, she has newfound
respect for him: having earlier taken him "por sot" ("for a
simpleton," 51), she now acknowledges his skill (61). Thereupon, the
story ends, without a moral pronouncement or any other form of
conclusion. The woman has learned her lesson, and it is a lesson that
may be all the more effective precisely because the narrator himself
does not insist on it.

As I suggested earlier, we cannot deduce from a few examples a
series of "rules" applicable to the corpus of fabliaux. Many fabliaux

---

[13] The introductory chapter deals briefly with the contents of this crude anecdote.

have little or nothing to do with women; certain others may not fit the "molds" we fashion for them. Yet, with this reservation in mind, we can summarize the general tendencies of many fabliau authors: 1) for the author, a man remains an individual, while a woman is regularly taken, implicitly or explicitly, as a representative of her sex; 2) the few exceptions to this statement (that is, the few cases in which generalizations are drawn from masculine behavior) point out the folly of trusting women, being controlled by them, or marrying them, the ultimate effect of such morals being to make unflattering implications about *women*; 3) whenever a fabliau author has a reasonable choice between two morals, critical respectively of men and of women, he chooses the latter; 4) a negative view of men, when it does occur and with whatever qualification, is likely to be followed by an additional moral that criticizes women.

In addition to the examples quoted above, a number of other fabliaux offer unequivocal condemnations of women, either in the morals or in brief authorial comments made in passing. We frequently learn of women's wiles: "fame set plus que deiable" ("women are better versed [in deceit] than the devil," *La Sorisete des estopes*, 214), and "molt set feme de renardie" ("women know many deceits," *Du Prestre et de la dame*, 172). We may be surprised to be told that a man is wrong to deceive a woman, but then we learn that this is wrong not implicitly, but rather because she will in return trick him ten or twenty times over (*Les Deux Changeors*, 286-87). We also hear a good deal about the carnal appetites of some women, and about their fickleness: *Du pescheor de pont seur Saine* assures us that if a woman had a man as great as Gauvain, and he were castrated, she would drop him in an instant in favor of the worst man of her household, "Por tant qu'ele le trovast tel / Qu'i la fotist bien et sovent" ("provided he would screw her often and well," 210-11). Men are considered foolish, in another fabliau, if they let women out at night (*Les Tresces*, 427-34). And the conclusion of *Auberee* offers an interesting, if qualified, defense of women: they would remain pure, we learn, if they were not led astray *by other women* (655-62).[14] In fact, that moral may recall to us the work with which we began, *De la dame escolliee*, in which the daughter's suffering is presented as the

---

[14] This is quoted from MR; the moral added to the fabliau is not included in Noomen's critical edition, but is present in five of the six manuscripts.

justifiable result of her improper behavior, which, in turn, is ultimately the fault of another woman.

Having considered a number of cases in which fabliau women appear as temptresses, corrupters, or corrupt, we should remind ourselves again that a great many fabliaux are not antifeminist—or profeminist, or even essentially *about* women. We should thus generalize with care, if at all. I am not at all certain that we can conclude that the fabliau genre itself is an essentially misogynistic form, if only because that would constitute an additional effort to cast all the fabliau texts in a single mold. On the other hand, we can with confidence note that a very considerable number of fabliaux are clearly and undeniably antifeminist.

Critical circumspection is required here, and detailed analyses of individual texts must replace the sort of wholesale generalizations that fill many manuals. I would suggest that it is neither possible nor particularly important to decide whether the fabliaux are more antifeminist, or less so, than other genres; nor is it crucial to distinguish the degree to which an author is inevitably reflecting the antifeminism of his culture or tradition from the degree of innovative misogyny his text incorporates. What *is* crucial in dealing with the fabliaux (whether about the "woman question" or another matter) is to recognize and respect the autonomy of individual texts. The idea of genre may depend on similarities, but the appeal of literature derives from differences, that is, from the uniqueness of texts.

In the fabliaux, we cannot expect to find feminist manifestos, and, to borrow Eichmann's statement again, it is clear that a good many fabliaux are "not favorable to women." But if it is a striking understatement to say that, in general, the authors of these works do not hold women in particularly high esteem,[15] it is also true that, in some fabliaux, questions of antifeminism are simply irrelevant. In others, poets may simply take for granted traditional assumptions regarding the proper role or the nature of women, or they may simply adopt those assumptions as part of the thematic stock in trade of fabliau authors. In such texts, attitudes toward women are significant—attitudes we are willing to accept, even for purposes of humor, tell us a good deal about a culture—but we should not assign

---

[15] Muscatine, however, does contend that *De un chivaler et de sa dame et de un clerk* "as a whole is almost profeminist in tone" (p. 123).

them to the same general category of "antifeminism" that we reserve for texts into which an author inserts categorical condemnations of women, or for those rare texts that present an unmistakable hatred of women behind a thin veil of humor. Whether our interest in this question is critical or ideological or both, our understanding of the fabliaux will increase as we systematically resist the temptation to homogenize the stories or the views they offer.

VI. Language in the Fabliaux

Text: *L'Esquiriel*

205 lines[1]
Noomen, VI, 33-49

*[A fifteen-year-old girl has been taught by her mother not to talk too much, because, the mother says, loquaciousness in a woman often leads to no good. In particular, her mother forbids her ever to pronounce the word designating the male organ. That proscription arouses the girl's interest, and she presses her mother until the latter reveals the name (*vit*); the word delights the girl and thus distresses the mother, who leaves weeping. A young man, having overhead the conversation, speaks with the girl, referring to his penis as a squirrel and his testicles as eggs laid in a nest by the squirrel. She asks if the animal eats nuts; hearing the affirmative reply, she laments the fact that she herself ate a large number of nuts the preceding day and thus has none to offer the animal. The man responds that the squirrel, by entering her body through her vagina, can look for them in her stomach. The creature searches everywhere for food, the result being orgasm (described as the squirrel weeping, then spitting, finally vomiting) and the man's prompt departure.]*

This text opens with lines hardly unexpected in a fabliau, although most fabliau authors would be less likely to have them spoken by female than by male characters or by the narrator: they are a mother's warning to her daughter against loquaciousness in a woman (16-27). The mother's particular concern is that her daughter never speak of "what men have hanging down" (25-27), although she does not explain the reason for this taboo. Predictably, the daughter is eager to know what she is forbidden to know, and she asks whether

---

[1] Noomen's last line is numbered 184, but between lines 27 and 29, his critical text includes lines numbered 27.1-27.21.

her mother is referring to the thing that hangs between her father's legs, indicating that she knows perfectly well what and where this thing is; she lacks only the name. Pressed to reveal the word, the mother first denies that it even has a name, then repeats that a woman should never name it.

The daughter continues to ask questions, but they become less direct and, indeed, almost nonsensical; eventually, the concealment of the proper name provokes such imaginative hypotheses ("is it a diver who swims in my father's fountain?" 30-33) that her mother yields to her entreaties and reveals that the name of the organ is *vit* (39). The young woman then reacts with delight, bursting into enthusiastic, almost orgiastic, repetition of the word: "I'll say 'prick,' my father says 'prick,' my sister says 'prick,' my brother says 'prick,' and even our chambermaid says 'prick,' a prick in front and a prick behind," and so on. The full passage is as follows:

> "Vit," dist ele, "Dieus merci, vit!
> Vit diré ge, cui qu'il anuit.
> Vit, chaitive! vit dit mon pere,
> Vit dist ma suer, vit dist mon frere,
> Et vit dist nostre chanberiere;
> Et vit avant et vit arriere,
> Vit dist chascuns a son voloir!
> Vos meïsmes, mere, por voir,
> Dites vit, et je, fole lasse,
> Qu'é forfet que vit ne nomasse?
> Vit a certes nomerai gié:
> Je meïsmes m'en doinz congié.
> Vit me doint Dieus que je n'i faille!" (43-55)

The implication—but it is an implication that will prove misleading—is that the linguistic taboo invests the word with far greater erotic force than it would have if the word were considered entirely neutral.

This fabliau, along with others that deal with the nature or force of language, will call to any medievalist's mind such discussions of language as the passage, well known and often discussed,[2] provided by Jean de Meun in the *Roman de la Rose*, after his character Reason refers to the testicles by the common word *coilles*. Pressed to justify the use of such a "vulgar" word, she insists that in fact it is not vulgar: it is not shameful to name "apertement par propre non" (6917) something created by God.[3]

Her interlocutor, L'Amant (The Lover), objects that, although God may have made the thing itself, he did not make the words, which are themselves disgraceful. The reply is that, if he did not make the words, he nonetheless gave to us, that is, to Reason, the duty of finding words that will identify things "proprement et conmunement" (7063). Reason then insists, in one of the most famous arguments in the *Rose*, that if she had called relics *coilles* and testicles *reliques*, Amant would surely condemn the word *reliques*. The words, she is saying, are *not* disgraceful; they themselves are neutral, and we attach to them our views of what they designate. Reason concludes, in a passage that could easily be taken as a gloss on the fabliau (or that makes of the fabliau a striking illustration of these lines), that *coilles* is a perfectly good word, and (7101-06) that if French women do not call them by their name, it is only by custom: if they learned to say it, they would find it pleasing and blameless.

This entire passage reflects a controversy as much in the thirteenth-century air as it has often been in that of the twentieth. Are words arbitrary constructs, or are they determined by what they designate? Can they be, in themselves, good or bad? L'Amant would undoubtedly side with the fabliau mother and her linguistic taboo, while Reason would surely find corroboration in the pleasure the young French woman takes in using the word. The passage in the *Rose* constitutes a defense of straightforward language, according to which one has the right, if not indeed the duty, to call a thing by its name. And the fabliau both confirms that view and offers an

---

[2] Most recently by Charles Muscatine, *The Old French Fabliaux* (New Haven: Yale University Press, 1986), pp. 146-50. See also Roy J. Pearcy, "Modes of Signification and the Humor of Obscene Diction in the Fabliaux," in *The Humor of the Fabliaux: A Collection of Critical Essays*, ed. Thomas D. Cooke and Benjamin L. Honeycutt (Columbia: University of Missouri Press, 1974), pp. 163-64.

[3] Guillaume de Lorris and Jean de Meun, *Le Roman de la Rose*, ed. Félix Lecoy (Paris: Champion, 1965-70), I, 212ff. (ll. 6915ff.).

illustration of what happens when one refuses to call a spade a spade—or a *vit* a *vit*.

In *L'Esquiriel*, it is curiosity not about genitalia, since the daughter already knows about those, but instead about language that arouses her interest and causes her to refer to the organ by a number of imaginative periphrases; and then, when she learns the word, she reacts gleefully, confirming about *vit* precisely what Reason had said of *coilles*: "Coilles est biaus nons et si l'ains" (7086): "it's a good word, and I like it."

At this point, the scene ends and another one begins, as her mother departs and the author mentions that a young man (Robin) has overheard their discussion. The relationship of the second half to the first presents an ostensible problem of narrative logic, to wit: since Robin knew of her joy at learning the word *vit*, what need was there to invent a euphemism, telling her that his penis was a squirrel (79)? Would he not logically assume that her delight at knowing the name would make her interested also in becoming better acquainted with the thing it designates?

The easy reaction would be to place blame for such a narrative problem on a clumsy redactor who, at some stage in the text's elaboration, made an ill-advised and illogical change, perhaps even fusing two anecdotes into one. Given the subsequent events of the tale, would it not have made far better narrative sense for the mother to withhold the name or, on the contrary, to reveal it only to have the daughter react with revulsion at the word? Had that happened, the use of a euphemism in the seduction attempt would have been justified (in the former case) or essential (in the latter).

The result in either instance would have been a very close analogue of such fabliaux as *La Damoiselle qùi ne pooit oïr parler de foutre* (see below, pp. 86-87). As it is, *L'Esquiriel*, by its implicit endorsement of direct and natural language, offers a narrative that is far more complex than that of *La Damoiselle qui ne pooit oïr parler de foutre*. The girl finds *vit* a good and pleasing word, but Robin's need to refer to his organ by another name suggests that her delight at the word *vit* is more linguistic than erotic; proof, if needed, is provided by my earlier citation, in which her reactions to the word entail explicit allusions to acts of language ("diré ge," "dit mon pere," "dist chascuns," "dites vit," "vit a certes nomerai gié"), but not of sex. The ordinary use of ordinary language empties it of erotic force, instead of increasing that force (as the mother apparently assumes). The word is no longer of utility in a seduction attempt.

On the other hand, it is apparent that Robin had observed the daughter's obvious talent for inventing metaphors (e.g., the diver in the fountain), and in fact the squirrel is far more metaphor than euphemism. Robin creates a metaphor with extraordinary potential for extension, and the girl follows his lead. Clearly, she is no less creative than he, and no careful reader of fabliaux could suppose that she took his words literally. Although many fabliaux are populated by characters of extraordinary naiveté,[4] there is no reason to believe that this one is. We have already seen that she knows what and where a penis is, lacking only a name for it, and we soon learn that she also knows *con*, both the word for it and what it is, for she has no trouble understanding his meaning when Robin suggests placing the squirrel into her *con* (130). She appears to have a more than adequate knowledge of human anatomy, and we must conclude consequently that she understands that the reference is a metaphor and chooses to play along.[5] To take her as victim or dupe is a misreading.

---

[4] In most cases, as in *L'Esquiriel*, it is a matter of a young woman whose naiveté, real or feigned (though it may not be in every instance possible to know which), makes her invite or accept a man's sexual attentions. An additional example, discussed in an earlier chapter, is *La Pucele qui voloit voler*. As the title indicates, a young woman wants to be able to fly and accepts a cleric's assistance in constructing a tail for her by means of copulation. The question "Is she really that naive?" is, as I indicated earlier, either irrelevant or unanswerable. Her "naiveté" is simply posited in order to allow for its consequences. In some fabliaux, however, naiveté appears to be an obvious pose. That seems to be true of *Aloul*, when the priest suggests that the woman breakfast on a particular vegetable with a large root and great medicinal value. She plays the game, though not on his rhetorical terms, by responding immediately, "open your legs and let me see" (82-84). Following their sexual interlude, the woman takes the role of the victimized innocent; the priest plays a similarly absurd role as her champion and courtly lover (100-07).

[5] A similar point is made by Pearcy, who notes that "no one appears to be victimized, and if the verbal manipulations constitute a trick, then it seems to be the hypocritically prudish side of one or both lovers' personalities that is deceived and circumvented, to their final mutual satisfaction." See Roy J. Pearcy, "Modes of Signification and the Humor of Obscene Diction in the Fabliaux," in *The Humor of the Fabliaux: A Collection of Critical Essays*, ed. Thomas D. Cooke and Benjamin L. Honeycutt (Columbia: University of Missouri Press, 1974), p. 77.

The events that follow his designation of his penis as a squirrel constitute both physical and rhetorical foreplay, in which both characters develop the metaphor at length and in detail. When the man refers to his testicles as eggs laid by the squirrel, she reacts without skepticism to that notion, implying, on first glance, that her knowledge of biology is seriously flawed (100ff.). But, in fact, her reaction tells us nothing about biology but much about her rhetorical skills and about the rhetorical games they are playing: its rules require her to respect even a defective metaphor. Part of the humor of this text derives from the absurdity of that metaphor, but not at all, to my mind, from any supposed naiveté on her part.

The exchange includes her invitation to the young man to have his squirrel look for nuts to eat. Muscatine reminds us that references to cracking, and presumably eating, nuts are a "vernacular synonym of *foutre*" (p. 140). He notes further that the image is "very vulgar," but what is most significant is that the vulgarity does not shock either of the characters: vulgarity becomes natural where natural language is considered vulgar. It is no longer a question of linguistic propriety or impropriety, but simply of linguistic indirection.[6] When verbal artifice replaces direct speech, the result can be illogical premises (e.g., squirrel eggs) or vulgarity (e.g., eating nuts) lurking just beneath the surface of sophisticated wordplay.

However, the larger point of this text, its real theme, is the erotic power of linguistic artifice: rhetoric, metaphor, euphemism. Language is dangerous: just as Ionesco tells us, in *La Leçon*,[7] that philology

---

[6] Here, it might appear that I differ with Bloch, who refers to these very passages from *L'Esquiriel* as a "set of verbal improprieties"; see Howard Bloch, *The Scandal of the Fabliaux* (Chicago: University of Chicago Press, 1986), p. 86. In the terminology I adopt, the question of impropriety does indeed become irrelevant, but I do not think my views are radically unlike those of Bloch, who uses "impropriety" to identify the result of "linguistic deflection." He does, however, draw a good many specific conclusions that I cannot accept. One is that *L'Esquiriel* "thematizes castration" (p. 78). Nor can I agree that the daughter's joy at hearing and using the word *vit* "eliminates the question of meaning altogether or reduces words to a pure phenomenon of sound" (p. 77); that contention implies (incorrectly, to my mind) that she would have reacted the same way regardless of what the word *vit* denoted—or even if it denoted nothing at all.

[7] In Eugène Ionesco, *Théâtre* (Paris: Gallimard, 1954), I, 89.

leads to crime, *L'Esquiriel* teaches us that rhetoric leads to sex.[8] Clearly, as I suggested, the mother's sense of propriety or her prudery provokes the daughter's delight in language more than in sex. Moreover, if simple and direct language provides intellectual interest rather than sexual arousal, linguistic *indirection* has the opposite effect. It is apparent that the desire to learn the name of "the thing men have hanging down" is in no way instrumental in the young woman's ritualized seduction—if, indeed, we can contend that *she was* seduced: Robin offered her an opportunity and the linguistic means of taking advantage of it, and she seized on both enthusiastically, playing as much a role as he in the preamble to sex. The result is at most mutual seduction.

One of the most striking observations we can make about this text, and also about other fabliaux that use metaphor or periphrasis to refer to sex organs and the act itself, is that the ensuing sex is far more graphic and violent than ordinary fabliau sex. And in most fabliaux, sex is indeed ordinary: intercourse is usually indicated by a simple formula or a direct statement, such as "il la fouta"; the erotic content of the narrative is minimal, and the act is straightforward and consequently uncomplicated.

In *L'Esquiriel*, however, the presumably heightened excitement, resulting from the verbal as well as physical foreplay, requires a more detailed description of the act, described with violent images that clash strongly with the rhetorical intricacy of the foreplay. Orgasm, as I noted, is described as the squirrel weeping, spitting, and vomiting (163-66), after which the woman expresses concern (170-72) that he may have broken one of the eggs (testicles).

An additional shock is produced by the conclusion of the narrative, which tells us in two matter-of-fact and apparently cynical lines (175-76) that, having finished, the man gets up, for there is nothing more to do. She invites him to repeat the search for nuts, but

---

[8] Linguistic indirection can also lead to serious *trouble* through sex, especially when a metaphor is lost on a literalistic mind. This is illustrated by *Celui qui bota la pierre*, in which a woman, talking to a priest in front of her house, idly kicks a stone. The priest warns her that if she does that again, he will take her immediately to bed ("je vous foutré," 24). She kicks it a second time, and he makes good on his "threat." When her husband later returns home, the couple's small child (who had witnessed the scene) warns his father, "Don't kick that stone, or our priest will fuck you just as he did my mother" (46-50).

he declines by noting that the squirrel no longer wants to, and the fabliau ends immediately and bluntly with "De cest fablel est ce la fins" (184).[9] That the conclusion is shocking in any way is itself revealing, but ironically so, because it too is entirely conventional. That is, in most fabliaux, the conclusion of the act is as routine as the act itself, and in those works, the simple statement that "he left when he was finished" sounds entirely natural. That same statement, however, becomes remarkable and implies correctly a cynical disregard for the woman when it follows a sex act almost as violent as a rape. There is no need for postcoital conversation here: no endearments, no thanks, not even, so far as we know, a good-bye.

MS. *A* appends a moral (201-06), not in the critical edition, that tells us that some may try to prevent a daughter from speaking foolishly but that the more one tries, the more one predisposes her to do evil.[10] While we might assume that the naming of parts predisposes her to sin with them, the situation, as both the seduction and the moral suggest, is far more complicated than that. Instead, Robin's linguistic indirection, his refusal to name parts (and presumably acts) by their simple and proper name, invests his metaphors with greater power and interest than would have been provided by the routine acceptance of the word *vit*.

*

---

[9] MS. *A* points out (199) that he immediately goes happily on his way. That line is absent from *B*, Noomen's base manuscript. On the other hand, *A* omits the woman's invitation to repeat the squirrel's search.

[10] *Cele qui fu foutue et desfoutue* is related to this manuscript by the insistence on a father's attempt to protect his daughter from worldly knowledge, and to *L'Esquiriel* in general by the use of a linguistic stratagem to accomplish a seduction. But the relationship of the two texts is not simple, and they are far from analogues. The man offers to trade a bird he has caught for a *foutre*. When the sheltered young woman protests that she does not have a *foutre* to give—only to have the man find one under her dress—we might presume that she is naive enough not to know the meaning of the word. However, the anecdote would be no less effective if she *did* know what she was saying, and this possibility can ultimately be neither proved nor disproved. The question belongs to the domain of the "undecidable" aspects of fabliaux (see Chapter IX).

Fabliaux that are closely related to this one include *La Dame qui aveine demandoit pour Morel sa provende avoir*, *Porcelet*, and especially *La Damoiselle qui ne pooit oïr parler de foutre*.[11] The last, one of the better-known "anti-prudery poems" (Muscatine, p. 141), involves a young woman who becomes violently ill when she hears the word *foutre*. A young man who knows her story pretends to share her affliction and is thus retained in her father's household. Very soon, the young people are exploring each other's bodies, but discussing their discoveries in metaphorical terms or, as Pearcy puts it, in a "nonce code."[12] This convenient approach confirms that her aversion was to the word but by no means to the act it designates nor to the agents by which the act is accomplished. That conclusion is illustrated when David's thirsty "colt," protected by two "guards" who are always with him, is invited to drink in the young women's "fountain."

This composition, though simpler than *L'Esquiriel*, plays doubly on matters of language. First, the father is not suspicious, because he equates the word with the deed: if the former is not said, the latter, he presumes, will not be done. But there are other ways to skin a cat, and the most effective way of all is, as in *L'Esquiriel*, by indirection,

---

[11] These same fabliaux are discussed by Bloch (pp. 83-90). As with the discussion of *L'Esquiriel* (see above), many of my conclusions are similar to Bloch's, although I would stop far short of relating the problems of these texts (or of many other fabliaux) to "the theme of castration writ so large across the genre as a whole" (p. 90).

[12] Roy J. Pearcy, "Investigations into the Principles of Fabliau Structure," in *Versions of Medieval Comedy*, ed. Paul G. Ruggiers (Norman: University of Oklahoma Press, 1977), p. 73. Pearcy notes that the young man is obviously not naive and that "future developments" suggest that the young woman is no more so. I depart from Pearcy's reading of this text only when he refers to their conversation as a collection of "ambiguous references." In the abstract, these may be ambiguous, but in the present context they are not: to the couple, they could hardly be clearer and less ambiguous. As my discussion of this text indicates, this and related fabliaux offer a system of lexical substitutions in which a character (or reader) who understands the principle cannot mistake the reference. Only in instances where the code is used in the presence of a potentially hostile character (e.g., a husband) must the code be ambiguous; that is the case for *Guillaume au faucon*, for *Du chevalier qui recovra l'amor de sa dame*, and especially for *La Saineresse*, but not for the "anti-prudery" fabliaux. (For a special case of ambiguous language, which a character takes as a threat of sodomy, see *Le Sot Chevalier*.)

through language and metaphor, allying rhetorical skills with physical desires to produce a ritualized seduction.

Yet, even in this simpler text, the question of euphemism or metaphor is not without complication. In one version of *La Damoisele qui ne pooit oïr parler de foutre* (MS. *D* of Noomen's edition, but entitled *La Pucele qui abreva le polain* in MR), the notion of the foal drinking at a fountain offers little that we have not already encountered. Nor does the text produce a surprise when the young woman asks her soon-to-be lover what his testicles are and he describes them, following the tradition of such fabliaux, not as *coilles*, but rather as two "marshals" or guards for his horse (193-94). Or, to be more precise, there would be no surprise except that the woman herself had already used the word *coilles*: in a curious and comically preposterous reference, she had identified her breasts as *coilles de mouton*, sheep's testicles. Why could the man not use the word when the woman had already done so? Muscatine (pp. 143-44) considers her use of a word forbidden to the man to be an "authorial slip" or confusion, an inadvertent lapse of the textual logic, and his conclusion is that "the word *coilles* did not carry much taboo in this author's milieu." That is, in one case the author censored it; in the other, he forgot to do so.

Muscatine may well be right about the author's milieu—the narrator himself had casually used the word *couillons* in line 190—but the fabliau is far less about that milieu than about the ethos of the text itself. In fact, the linguistic taboo actually carries *more* force here than in most of the so-called "anti-prudery" fabliaux; it does not simply permit, but in a curious way fosters, the apparent aberration noted by Muscatine. The taboo proscribes not a particular word, but a *way of using language*. That is, almost as a matter of principle, it imposes a system of lexical substitutions and outlaws *every* word that simply and directly designates an object or organ. It is not simply a question of euphemistically naming that which ought not be said, but instead a matter of metaphorical language in which *everything* must be given another name. Thus, in this system, the characters must not call testicles *coilles*, but in a kind of euphemistic inversion, there is nothing to prevent them from using that word metaphorically for any anatomical features that are *not* testicles. To my mind, this passage, far from being a "slip" or confusion, serves, better than any other fabliau example, to illustrate the absurdity to which linguistic indirection can lead us.

La Dame qui aveine demandoit pour Morel sa provende avoir offers a dual focus, one of them on language but the dominant one on the presumed natural subservience of women to men. The principal point the work makes is that it is in the interest of men and women alike for the former to dominate relationships. The narrator could easily enough have made that point without the emphasis on metaphor, but it is surely significant that a reversal of what he takes as the natural order is accompanied if not provoked by a linguistic perversion.

The fabliau has a man delegate to his wife the authority to decide when they will have sex, and the title refers to a formula he wants her to use as a signal: Morel (a name for a horse) needs some oats. Obviously, the husband finds it acceptable for a woman to "do it," but not to call "it" by its usual name. That is a linguistic taboo, not unknown in our own century, that calls to mind the dictum "mout a entre faire et dire" ("there is a great difference between saying and doing," 229 of *La Pucele qui abreva le polain*, MS. *D* of *La Damoisele qui ne pooit oïr parler de foutre*). And certainly, the fabliau implies, it is improper for the wife to dictate when it is to be done. The husband's error, as subsequent events prove, is in giving her the authority to decide such things. But it is interesting that the transfer of power is accompanied by a linguistic transformation: the shift away from "proper" sex roles includes a related shift away from ordinary language, the good and proper words endorsed by Jean de Meung's Reason, to metaphorical diction presumed to be free of impropriety but in fact intimately related to the near-destruction of the couple's marriage.

Curiously, the couple's affliction is cured when, no longer capable of performing upon command, he responds to a request for Morel's oats by defecating on his wife and informing her that the oats are exhausted (as it were) and that this is all Morel will have from now on. This distasteful act shifts authority back to him, as the creation of the Morel metaphor had given it to her.

There are, as Muscatine points out (p. 129), other fabliaux in which excrement is presented as the alternative to sex or to semen. However, *Morel*, like many fabliaux, is a more complex creation than a first reading might suggest. Its point involves the destruction or distortion of what should be pleasurable and natural, and in this text "natural" refers both to sexual relations unencumbered by linguistic artifice and to the rejection of female dominance. That is, *Morel* not only hinges on the opposition of excrement to the natural relations (including sexual ones) between men and women, but also implies complex connections between excrement and language, specifically because the perversion of the couple's relations is emblematized in a linguistic perversion.

Porcelet offers a simplified analogue of *Morel*, but with the humor nicely enhanced by a pun. In this text, the wife gives names not to the sex act but to their organs: hers is Porcelet ("Little Pig") and his is Fromant ("Wheat"). Thus, whenever the piglet is hungry, it can be fed wheat until it is satisfied. Eventually, though, the husband suffers crop failure (35) and is no longer able to provide the proper nourishment; when asked to perform, he passes wind instead (". . . lait aler un pet / El giron a la damoisele," 38-39). Asked what that was, he responds that he had spread *bran* to be eaten by the pig. *Bran* is bran, the husks of wheat left after the milling process, but it also means "excrement." That, he says, is all that is left of the wheat, for he is not only defeated, but "de-wheated" (*desfromantez*, 56).

In the context of these last two fabliaux, it is surely pertinent to call attention to the frequency of scatological themes—excrement and flatulence—in medieval comic literature, from *Morel* and *Porcelet* to *Jouglet* and Rutebeuf's *Pet au vilain*[13] to the parody of *Audigier*

---

[13] In fact, *Le Pet au vilain* may be, among the texts mentioned here, the one that best explains the use and meaning of anal functions in the fabliaux. In both literary and pictorial art of the Middle Ages, we often find the soul leaving the dying body through the mouth. The obverse of this situation has the damned soul departing through the anus. Thus, in *Le Pet au vilain* the peasant's fart is mistaken for his soul; devils take it back to hell in a bag and release it, to the intense displeasure of all. (That is why peasants are no longer welcome in hell.) Flatulence and excrement, as this story illustrates, are associated with perversions in general; that they are often emblematic of linguistic perversions in particular surely underlines the crucial importance the Middle Ages attached to the word and the speech act, intimately associated with the nature of the human soul. Incidentally, Rutebeuf's conclusion to this fabliau explicitly relates it to *Audigier* and to "la terre de Cocuce, / Ou Audigiers chie en s'aumuce" (Audigier's "land of Cocuce, where Audigier shits in his hat" or hood); see n. 14.

(where the connection is of excrement to epic formulas).[14] However, what is most important here is not the simple appeal of scatology, but specifically its fundamental relationship to speech. That relationship is dramatically illustrated by a fabliau like *Du con qui fu fait a la besche*, which explains woman's tendency to chatter nonsense: the devil, after fashioning Eve's sex organs, then farted on her tongue ("Un pet li a fet sor la langue," 65).[15] Equally dramatic is Chaucer's *Miller's Tale*, in which Absolon invites conversation; he says "Spek, swete byrd" and receives instead "a fart, as greet as it hadde been a thonder dent" (3806-07).[16] Moreover, the link between linguistic perversion and scatology is established not only in the down-to-earth comedy of the fabliaux and Chaucer, but also in that most serious of comedies: the *Divine Comedy*. We have only to recall that in Dante's *Inferno* (Canto XVIII) the flatterers, perverters of language, are submerged in excrement, reflecting, as one of them (Alessio Interminei) states, "the flatteries of which my tongue never tired."[17]

---

[14] For the text and a brief (and embarrassed) discussion of the convergence of epic formulas and scatology, see Omer Jodogne, "Audigier et la chanson de geste, avec une nouvelle édition du poème," *Le Moyen Age*, 66 (1960), 495-526. See, for example, the description of the personal habits of Audigier's father Sir Turgibus, 11-13, or of his mother Rainberge, 61-62. Perhaps surprisingly, *Audigier* has been little studied. It is, however, one of the four "parodic" texts examined by Kathryn Gravdal in *Vilain and Courtois: Transgressive Parody in French Literature of the Twelfth and Thirteenth Centuries* (Lincoln: University of Nebraska Press, 1989). See also the perceptive essay, by Judith M. Davis, "*Audigier* and the Poetics of Scatology," in *Poetics of Love in the Middle Ages*, ed. Moshe Lazar and Norris J. Lacy (Fairfax: George Mason University Press, 1989), pp. 237-48.

[15] Thus, this text attributes to the devil both a woman's sexuality—God, having forgotten to form her vagina, delegated that responsibility to the devil—and her incessant talk.

[16] Quoted from Thomas W. Ross, ed., "The Miller's Tale." A Variorum Edition of the Works of Geoffrey Chaucer, vol. 2, pt. 3 (Norman: University of Oklahoma Press, 1983), p. 240.

[17] *Inferno*, XVIII, 103-26; esp. 125-26: "Qua giú m'hanno sommerso le lusinghe / ond' io non ebbi mai la lingua stucca." See Natalino Sapegno, ed., *La divina commedia* (Florence: "La Nuova Italia," 1963), p. 213. The pertinence of this passage to my discussion was suggested to me by Christopher Kleinhenz.

*

During the Middle Ages as now, the erotic power of language is taken for granted; the preceding fabliaux illustrate that power, and they also demonstrate specifically the destructive effect of linguistic perversion. But if language used improperly in the fabliaux can engender sexual violence, corrupt young women, and disrupt marriages, it can also, when used intelligently, prove to be the most effective means of exercising power or imposing one's desires on others. That observation is borne out by several fabliaux that are quite different in nature from those discussed above. I will complete my examination with three fabliaux, one of them dealing with sex, the second with death, the last with life after death.

The first is one of the briefest and cleverest of erotic fabliaux, *Du prestre ki abevete*. As a *vilain* and his wife are having dinner, a priest who is attracted to the wife arrives and observes them through a hole in the door. Speaking to them through the door, he accuses them of copulating rather than eating ("vous foutez!"). When the husband denies it, the priest tells him that dining certainly looks like sex when you watch it from outside, and he challenges the husband to come out and see for himself. The husband goes outside, and the priest enters and immediately begins to do to the wife "that thing that women like most" (57-58). When the priest assures the *vilain* that he is now dining with the woman, the husband replies that it does indeed appear that they are indulging in sex, concluding, "If I had not heard you say it, I would never have believed that you were not screwing my wife" (72-73). The priest responds that, yes, he had the same impression a few minutes earlier.

This fabliau is very short—eighty-four lines—but is rather less simple than it may appear. It involves less the naiveté of the husband than the persuasive power of language; or, rather, we might say that the *subjects* are the man's naiveté and the seduction, but the *theme* is the authority of language. While we might expect to hear characters say, "I wouldn't have believed it if I hadn't seen it with my own eyes," such trust in visual perception is overturned in favor of a

greater confidence placed in the spoken word.[18] Things may be taken
as the exact opposite of what they appear to be, simply because they
are said to be so. Nor does this fabliau suggest that the words carry
more weight because they are those of a priest; the narrator does not
imply that, and what we know of fabliau priests does not inspire
confidence that their words are implicitly accepted. It is the weight of
language, and not the authority of the speaker, that establishes the
innocence of activities inside the house.

In a fabliau like *Le Vilain de Bailluel*, language has even greater
power: it can persuade a man that he is dead. When a man
announces that he is dying of hunger (32), his wife seizes on the
occasion, agrees with him, and soon insists that he *is* dead.
Thereupon, she indulges in a dalliance with the priest, before the very
eyes of the husband, who, because he is dead, is powerless to
interfere. This fabliau has a good deal in common with *Du prestre ki
abevete*: both involve sex between a wife and a priest, at the expense
of her naive husband, but, most important, both depict the utility of
language in facilitating the dalliance.

It is true that *Le Vilain de Bailluel* plays more heavily on the
husband's naiveté and on the contrast of literal and figurative
language, rather than on that of language and perception. Yet, at one
level, the point is the same: words do have weight and meaning, and
they are capable of performing what neither reason nor visual
perception can accomplish. It is not that the husband has no
conception of figurative language, for it was he who first referred in
figurative terms to his dying; rather, the force of the words is such
that when his wife transposes them to the literal level, he follows suit.
The retreat from figurative language to literal meaning multiplies the
power of the word.

Again, I am not arguing that the man is not colossally naive and
stupid—that is the major element of the fabliau's humor—but that the
instrumentality revealing his stupidity involves the irresistible force of
the word he utters, only to find it wielded as a weapon by his wife.

---

[18] *Le Chevalier a la robe vermeille*, for example, insists that the person is foolish
"qui croit ce que de ses iex voie" ("who believes what he sees with his own eyes,"
314). The narrator goes on to say, in what Schenck describes as "a blatantly sarcastic
moral" (30), that a man should instead always believe everything his wife tells him
(316-17).

The same play on literal and figurative language occurs elsewhere in the fabliau corpus, most obviously in *Brunain la vache au prestre* and *La Vieille qui oint la palme au chevalier*, but in none does the weight of language play as heavy a role as in *Le Vilain de Bailluel*.

Not only can language produce and conceal sexual activity and persuade a man that he is dead, it can also provide the key to salvation. *Du vilain qui conquist paradis par plait* is one of the simplest of fabliaux; indeed, it is a text that some might exclude from the fabliau corpus, or at least situate on its periphery, because the thrust of the composition is moralizing rather than comical. Nonetheless, it is an exceedingly well-constructed text, and it is in particular one of the clearest examples of the power of language in the fabliaux.

After the man's death, curiously, neither angels nor devils come to take charge of his soul. Although this fact is not explained, it is an appropriate event, as it leaves him to his own devices. His soul sees St. Michael leading another soul to heaven, and decides to follow. Arriving at the gates of heaven, he is required to talk his way in. The rest of the text presents the intelligence and perspicacity with which he does so.

The word *vilain*, referring to one's station in life but also used by the saints as a reference to base character, occurs nearly a dozen times in this 172-line text. It is most often uttered by one of the saints in question, who contrast their virtue and nobility to his lack of distinction; they insist that heaven is reserved for those who have been martyred or have confessed (57), and St. Thomas refers to the place as the "maizons as cortois" (61), the dwelling of the courtly or faithful.

The man's soul rebukes St. Peter for having denied Christ three times, whereas he himself had been "prodom et loiaus" ("worthy and faithful," 44). Next, he reminds Thomas that he doubted his Lord (69-71) and that he therefore should not reside in heaven. He then criticizes Paul as a cruel tyrant who had St. Stephen stoned (90-93) and caused the death of many another man. Paul tells Peter and Thomas how he has been bettered by the *vilain*, adding that in his opinion the soul has earned admittance. The three go before God, where Peter admits that "Par parole nos a vaincus" (117), *"by his words* he defeated us."

God speaks with the soul, pointing out that the latter has vilified and criticized His apostles. In response, the soul insists that *he* never denied or doubted the Lord, nor did he ever kill anyone. He adds a description of his own virtuous and kind life (137-52), noting that he gave to the poor, sheltering and clothing them and denying them nothing they needed. After this description, which offers definite echoes of the Sermon on the Mount, he concludes the argument with two points: he notes that God himself had promised that anyone who died following such a virtuous life would have his sins forgiven (153-54) and that—the clincher—no one who had once entered heaven would be sent away (159-60).

In the key line of this fabliau, God responds that the soul has presented his case so well that he has won his point, for "bien ses avant metre ta verbe!" (165, "you surely know how to advance your argument"). The author adds a moral to point out that many a man demands something when he could instead have won it through speech (167-68) and that cleverness is of more value than force (172).

Although the text makes it clear on several occasions that it is the soul's skill in the use of language that wins the day, that fact is easy to overlook, if only because we tend to bring other expectations to the text. Pointing out the sins of the saints and contrasting them to his own virtuous life, the soul argues that he is more deserving than they. Indeed, he is, since we have no reason to question his evaluation of himself, but the conclusive point is the merit not of his life but of his argumentation. It is not his virtue, but *la verbe*, speech or language used properly, that earns himself a place in heaven. The power of language prevails.[19]

If we begin to examine individual fabliaux, we find that a great many of them turn, one way or another, on questions of language. Some of them are mere puns (*Estula*), while others deal with dialectal or foreign pronunciations (*De deux angloys et de l'anel*). Many of them deal with seduction accomplished by linguistic means rather than pure desire. Several exploit the difference between literal and figurative language, although not always in the way we anticipate. And, as demonstrated in this chapter, a good many depend for their

---

[19] This text and most of those preceding illustrate Schenck's observation that "the performatory power of language . . . makes reality rather than merely reflecting it" (p. 101).

effect on questions of metaphor. In one way or another, they illustrate beyond any doubt the preoccupation of fabliau authors with language and its relation to sexuality, the natural hierarchy of the sexes, power, and authority. Whereas I have noted in another chapter that the fabliaux are narratives about narration, it is also correct to conclude that, even before that, they are fundamentally language about language.

VII. The Narrator's Voice

Text: *Estormi*

By Hues Piaucele
630 lines
Noomen, I, 1-28

[Three priests, who have designs on a woman, offer her money in exchange for sexual favors. She informs her husband of their intentions, and they conceive a plan whereby they can have the money and yet protect the woman's honor: the husband hides in the house and then kills each of the priests in turn. The three are buried one after the other by the man's nephew Estormi, who takes them all to be a single corpse that escapes from its grave and requires reinterment. Finally, on his way home, he meets a priest on the road, and, outraged that the body has escaped once again, he kills him with his shovel and buries him beside the others.]

This fabliau is a reworking of the motif known as the "corpse many times killed" or, more precisely in this case, many times buried.[1] Interestingly, although plot summaries generally dilute or destroy humor, the opposite is true in *Estormi*: the humor of this story is much more in evidence in a brief retelling than in a reading of the full fabliau. The reason for that, surely, is that in a reading the intrigue or anecdote is virtually lost, submerged under the signs of self-conscious narration. Although it is by no means uncommon for fabliau narrators to intervene freely, we would surely be hard-pressed

---

[1] A very close analogue of this story is offered by *Les Trois Boçus*, in which a woman hides three hunchbacks of whom her husband is jealous. They suffocate in their hiding places, and one by one the woman has them dumped in the river, using fundamentally the same stratagem as the couple in *Estormi*. Finally, the perplexed dupe who is disposing of the bodies comes upon the woman's own husband, who happens to be a hunchback himself, and kills him.

to find one as visible and self-conscious as the narrator of *Estormi*. This narrator is remarkable in two ways: first, for offering a running commentary on his material and his own technique; second, for proving himself as inept as he is obvious. Not only intrusive but seriously befuddled, he is the model of the incompetent storyteller, forgetting essential information, then thinking of it and adding it at an inappropriate time. My contention, however, is not that he is incapable of effective narration, but rather that his design, which is evidently to depict (and spoof?) the narrative process, includes the creation of a dramatized inept storyteller.[2]

In addition to inserting several pointless digressions that blunt the effect, the narrator frequently comments both on the story and on his own telling of it. Regarding the story itself, he assures us more than once that he is telling it just as his source (the "livre" or "matière," 21, 28, 29) preserved it and that we will hear it all if we listen patiently. He confesses when he does not know something: he is not certain how the formerly rich couple became poor, "Quar onques conté ne me fu: / Por ce ne le doi pas savoir" ("because no one ever explained it to me, for which reason I cannot be expected to know," 10-11).

After the priests are killed, but before they are buried, the woman decides to look for Estormi, and the narrator offers a double digression. He has the couple discuss whether Estormi is in the brothel or the tavern (266-72). He is in the tavern, playing dice and (we are told) losing. We witness a conversation between the woman and the proprietor concerning the young man's losses, and the woman pays them. The second digression, following from this one, deals with the dangers of gambling, and the narrator challenges us to ask someone else if we do not believe him (284-85). Suddenly, he stops short, says that this is not part of his story ("Mais ne vueil mie plus tenir / Ceste parole . . ."; "But I don't want to talk any more about that," 288-89), and changes the subject, revealing to us the young man's name—"a non Estormis" (307)—as though for the first time, even though we have known the name since the beginning.

---

[2] I use the term "dramatized" hesitantly here, since a dramatized narrator is traditionally one who is a character in the text. My contention here is that the narrator interposes himself into the work with such insistence and prominence that he virtually becomes the focus of his own narration.

Another digression follows the denouement, when the narrator adds a rambling moral and then the gratuitous information that Estormi had dinner with his relatives, and his uncle kept him company, "Mes je ne sai mie combien / Il furent puisse di ensamble" ("But I don't know how long they were together," 618-19).

Concerning his own narrative method, he gives himself "stage directions," such as "Or est resons que je vous die / De Jehan" ("Now it is proper for me to tell you about Jehan," 418-19), and he remarks that

> Or sai je bien qu'il me covient
> Dire par quel reson Jehans,
> Qui mout ot cele nuit d'ahans,
> Remist les deus prestres ensamble.
> Se ne le vous di, ce me samble,
> Li fabliaus seroit corrompus

("I realize that I must now tell why Jehan, who had suffered greatly that night, placed the two bodies together; if I don't tell you, I think the fabliau will be ruined," 250-55)

Finally, in the most remarkable of many signs of both self-consciousness and ineptitude, he interjects, as might someone who tells jokes badly, "Oublié avoie une chose" ("I forgot to tell you one thing," 135). Thereupon, and far too late, he explains that the lady had lured the priests to her home by suggesting that her husband was away.

Obviously, whether this narrator is incompetent in reality or, as I believe, systematically affecting incompetence,[3] he suffers from a severe professional inadequacy. At every turn, he calls our attention to his self-consciousness and, more to the point, to his deficiencies.

---

[3] When I speak of an incompetent narrator, I am talking of narratorial personas. That is, I am not necessarily implying that the narrator *cannot* tell a story well—although some clearly cannot—but only that he chooses not to do so and that that inability is a component of the humor. One inevitably wonders whether the interventions of *Estormi* are the creation of a redactor-scribe, but, unfortunately, that cannot be determined, since the text is extant in a single manuscript. In any event, they present a bumbling narrator in a way we might expect in an oral performance, but hardly in the manuscript record of such a performance.

He is not only visible but extraordinarily insecure. His ineptitude progressively and persuasively dismantles his own narrative authority but, remarkably, leaves the independence and authority of the anecdote intact. In fact, in a curious way it reaffirms them, as will references to extraneous material in other fabliaux as well (see below). Part of this affirmation is explicit, of course, as he refers to the book containing his subject matter and tells us what is and is not included therein. More significant, however, are his reflections on, and indictments of, his own artistry; for while the signs of inept oral presentation undermine the humorous appeal of the fabliau, they also confirm our conviction that there is indeed an amusing story there—if only the narrator could manage to get it right. The tale remains independent from the teller; the messenger is not to be confused with his message and is responsible not for its content, but only for the effectiveness (or here, the ineffectiveness) of its delivery.

The narrative technique in this fabliau surely gives the lie to a good many traditional assumptions. For example, years ago, Walter Morris Hart pronounced the fabliaux "the best narrative art of the Middle Ages."[4] After Hart, others (myself included) either said or implied that the fabliaux exhibit something akin to organic unity, that they typically contain everything necessary and nothing extraneous and that every line is carefully crafted to serve the purposes of narrative economy and effectiveness. There is in this praise a certain scholarly condescension, the implication being that the fabliaux do not try to do very much, but what they do, they do well. And, perhaps with the same condescension, scholars have often agreed: the narrative excellence of the fabliaux, within a framework of diminished expectations, has often been beyond rebuke.

Now, as I reread certain fabliaux, I wonder whether Hart and all the others—including myself—had actually read carefully in the first place. The kind of judgment I referred to is not easily reconciled with the activity of narrators who, in a good many instances, provide distracting or irrelevant commentary, admit their own inadequacy, or simply botch their job. A proper appreciation of these texts requires a fresh reading, unencumbered by the critical baggage provided by

---

[4] "The Fabliau and Popular Literature," *PMLA*, 23 (1908), 329-74.

Hart, Bédier,[5] and—lest I appear to be beating a dead critical horse—most recent critics as well. Desiderata of fabliau scholarship would constitute a long list of items, but near the top would surely be an assessment of the variety and vitality of fabliau narration.

"Instead of a fable I will tell you a true story," announces one of the numerous narrators who emphasize the veracity of their fabliaux. Despite his assurances, however, we will surely question his contention and the truth of his story (*Cele qui se fist foutre sur la fosse de son mari*; see chapter I) if we recognize the tale as a close analogue of a traditional narrative known as the Matron of Ephesus, descended from Petronius and other sources and known in a number of versions in Old French. And if any doubts remain concerning the truth of these texts, it will suffice for us to read a fabliau by an author named Guerin, who solemnly assures us that he *never* lies—and then introduces a man whose principal gift is the ability to make female genitalia talk (*Le Chevalier qui fist parler les cons*, 12).[6]

These two fabliaux offer typical assurances that could be multiplied many times over and whose function surely merits

---

[5] See Joseph Bédier, *Les Fabliaux: études de littérature populaire et d'histoire littéraire du moyen âge* (Paris, 1894; 6th ed., Paris: Champion, 1964). Bédier calls the fabliaux "la littérature des indigents," in which "le rire y est singulièrement facile" and which the audience enjoyed "comme des enfants" (pp. 311, 310). He insists on the "absence de toute prétention littéraire" (p. 341), criticizes their "poétique très rudimentaire" (p. 342), and concludes that these "petites comédies" hardly merited wasting "de beaux feuillets de parchemin" (p. 341). "Tel est bien le caractère essentiel des fabliaux: le poète ne songe qu'à dire vitement et gaiement son conte, sans prétention, ni recherche, ni vanité littéraire. De là ses défauts: négligence de la versification et du style, platitude, grossièreté. De là aussi des mérites, parfois charmants: élégante brièveté, vérité, naturel" (p. 347). He goes on damning with faint praise: "Avec une entière bonne foi, la grossièreté du style suit la grossièreté du conte." The key to all this is Bédier's conviction that the fabliaux were bourgeois literature, amusing but simple and unsubstantial compositions appropriate for their public.

[6] For the Middle Ages, "truth" often refers not to that which is factual, but rather to something that has exemplary value. In this instance, though, it is not easy to locate the exemplary value of the anecdote, and that very fact may be part of the humorous appeal of the fabliau.

attention.[7] The truth of fabliaux is, of course, a patent fiction, a simple convention of humorous narrative,[8] and besides depicting events that strain our credulity beyond the breaking point, the very authors who assure us that their stories are true curiously make only the most perfunctory efforts, if any at all, to support their contentions. At most, we find a general reference to geography and time (in the first example given above, "Flandre" and "jadis"), and beyond that the author, unconcerned with the kind of specificity that might reinforce his claims, contributes to their dismantling.[9]

But the fact that the claims are without substance does not mean that they are also without effect. By making such claims, and by referring frequently to their written or oral sources, authors are emphasizing that what I will call the anecdote (that is, the sequence of events to be presented, or, to borrow Genette's term, the *histoire*[10]) is not of their making, that they are appropriating and presenting a preexistent narrative. Such assertions are among the ways narrators define their compositional responsibility, which in the fabliaux extends only to presentation, and not to substance or fact. In other words, they are affirming, as an element of their artistic activity, a systematic disjunction between the anecdote and its presentation (or, again in Genette's terms, between the *histoire* and the *récit*, pp. 71-72).

Here, as with many other questions concerning the fabliaux, a parallel with the joke proves instructive. In both the fabliau and the joke, the status of the material is privileged, either as reputedly—but *only* reputedly—factual (example: "this really happened to a friend of

---

[7] Roger Dubuis devotes considerable detail to the question of "l'authenticité des faits" in the fabliaux. See his *"Les Cent Nouvelles Nouvelles" et la tradition de la nouvelle en France au moyen âge* (Grenoble: Presses Universitaires de Grenoble, 1973), pp. 143-59.

[8] See Richard O'Gorman, ed., *Les Braies au cordelier* (Birmingham: Summa, 1983), p. 118: ". . . such an insistence on the 'truth' of what will turn out to be a humorously improbable (and in some fabliaux impossible) story amounts to that sort of discrepancy which contributes to the comic effect of the tale."

[9] See Dubuis, p. 148.

[10] Gérard Genette, *Figures III* (Paris: Seuil, 1972), pp. 71-72.

mine") or as clearly fictional but nonetheless preexistent material that the teller chooses to relate. The narrator has considerable freedom in his introductory and concluding remarks and any interventions, with his purposes and his narrative skills serving as the only restraints; but his methods, including frequent comments on sources and his treatment of them, constitute tacit or even explicit acknowledgment of the essential autonomy of the anecdote. His skill may enhance the presentation or the effect of the joke or tale, just as his possible ineptitude would compromise it; neither, however, influences the author's or audience's perception of that autonomy.

Admittedly, there is really nothing very remarkable, especially for medievalists, in the implicit distinction made by fabliaux between textual autonomy and narrative authority. In fact, in regard to the fabliaux and to a good many other forms, the distinction is axiomatic. The anecdotes *were* generally, if not always, preexistent material circulating orally or in written form or, very often, both. Yet authors of fabliaux generally cultivate this disjunction, rather than simply acknowledge or even ignore it; indeed, far from trying to integrate the *histoire* seamlessly into their *récit*, their narrators typically affirm and even privilege its independence, its status as a received anecdote or body of material.

The relationship of the fabliau narrator to his material remains problematic, however, doubtless because theorists and critics have customarily fashioned narrative categories that can account for postmedieval, but not medieval, literary composition. Genette, for example, imposes a distinction (pp. 71-72) between events that are considered "real" and whose status is entirely independent of their narrative presentation, and material that is clearly fictive, a status that privileges the narrative act on which it depends for its existence. We would likely assign fabliaux to the former category were it not that we recognize their truth claims as fictions, not to be taken literally: many fabliau situations were not, and could not have been, "real." In fact, we can say *neither* that fabliau anecdotes are real nor, in most cases, that they are a function of authorial creation. Clearly, the fabliaux will require an additional category.

If Genette's theories are of limited applicability to medieval literature in general, the same can be said of narrative categories devised by a good many other critics. Susan Sniader Lanser's *The*

Narrative Act: Point of View in Prose Fiction,[11] for example, deals specifically with the question of authority in literature, dividing it into diegetic authority attached to the authorial voice and mimetic authority generated by the actors in the work. But her categories, too, fail to account for the particularities of medieval literary composition.

Medieval texts are often authenticated neither by the reality or factual truth of their content, nor by their own authors' narrative acts, but by their association with other texts and their participation in a larger narrative tradition.[12] *Auctoritas*, the "authority" that provides authentication of a medieval work, derives, as E. Jane Burns says, "from the citation of previous texts, and the validity of an author's literary contribution lies less in his ingenious rendition of the subject matter than in the ability to align his text with those of previous authors."[13] Although *auctoritas* originally referred to the authority that attached to classical authors (*auctores*) deemed worthy of study and citation,[14] the notion soon expanded, in practice if not in theory, to confer value on any text—even an unwritten text—that might be used to authenticate, in turn, the text being composed or studied. In the Arthurian Vulgate Cycle discussed by Burns, the narrators refer repeatedly to a *conte*, which is not a specific account but rather the entire tradition, textually nonexistent but no less real, on which the Arthurian romances repose.

---

[11] (Princeton: Princeton University Press, 1981).

[12] Obviously, these phenomena considerably complicate questions of narrative point of view in medieval literature, for the narrator often functions merely as the transmitter of material. Point of view is rendered yet more complex in very short narratives, where (for example) reader "identification" with characters is generally precluded by the nature of the text. In this chapter, I focus primarily on direct narratorial interventions, but throughout the volume I have made observations that are pertinent to questions of point of view; examples include misleading generic designations, internal contradictions of fact or interpretation, and even the use of the kind of stock characters (e.g., lascivious priests) that generate specific expectations on the part of the audience.

[13] E. Jane Burns, *Arthurian Fictions: Rereading the Vulgate Cycle* (Columbus: Ohio State University Press, 1985), p. 40.

[14] See A.J. Minnis, *Medieval Theory of Authorship* (Missoula: Scolar Press, 1984; 2nd ed., Philadelphia: University of Pennsylvania Press, 1988), esp. pp. 1-15.

In a good many examples from a variety of medieval texts, the invocation of authority was vague, as an author tells us that "the authorities say . . ." but without naming them; and sometimes texts may cite authorities who do not exist or who do exist but never said what is attributed to them. The point of all this is to emphasize that, for the Middle Ages, literary authority may reside partly in the narrative act and in the mimetic activity within texts, but it also resides elsewhere, in the authority of precedent texts, existent or imaginary.

The fabliaux are, however, a specific case, because the authenticating texts are not distinct literary works, but simply precedent versions of the anecdotes being related. Their very preexistence, the fact that the stories have been told before, provides sufficient authority for their proliferation.[15] In a culture in which texts are most often shared or appropriated or adapted, we cannot be surprised at the fabliaux' insistence on their status as pre-existent narratives, but the consequence is that the text as source is used as the means of authenticating the same text as product. The text in effect validates itself, and the truth claims or references to sources serve the same fundamental, aesthetic purpose as would the invocation of theological or classical *auctoritas* in a different kind of work.

In turn, recognition of the autonomy of the fabliau anecdote has significant implications. Quite obviously, it splits narrative authority in half, and, as I suggested, the author and his narrator retain responsibility simply for presentation. The distancing of the narrative voice from the matter to be recounted confers upon authors extraordinary creative freedom in regard to their narrative methods and procedures. But contrary to our expectations, that freedom very often does not produce the finely hewn comic structures that we have traditionally associated with the fabliaux.

Instead, the result is in many cases an overt methodological experimentation, including the crafting of strategies that may either build or undermine our confidence in the narrative skill of the

---

[15] I thus disagree on this point with Dubuis, who argues (p. 151) that fabliau authors are entirely unconcerned with authenticating their stories. Admittedly, they do not customarily go to great lengths to do so, but the need for authority requires at least a brief and conventional response.

authors.[16] It may produce an effective and economical story, but it just as often explains the diversity and illogic of some textual commentary and the creation and dramatization of widely divergent narrative personas, including more than a few that present themselves as hopelessly incompetent.

These suggestions contradict traditional assumptions, mentioned earlier, concerning the economy and effectiveness of fabliau composition. It is undeniable that a good many fabliaux are indeed stripped of all inessential material, and a few are even conspicuous by the starkness of their composition. Others, though longer and more complex, still present an anecdote largely unencumbered by intrusive commentary, offering at most the traditional announcement that a fabliau is forthcoming, an occasional remark of the "ço cuit" ("I believe") variety, and perhaps a brief moral, often serving less as didactic reflection than as a simple sign of closure.

In some cases, more extensive authorial commentary, far from being a liability, instead contributes to narrative effectiveness. It is customary, for example, for the author simply to inform us that a character is stupid or deceitful or lascivious. Such compression and authorial intrusions, while violating the Jamesian stricture against telling instead of showing, clearly serve the interests of humor and efficient narration.

Yet, if some fabliau authors have their narrators restrict their commentary to unexceptional observations and to the establishment of character, others exhibit a remarkable range of intrusions and digressions. Those intrusions may, as we have seen, constitute truth claims or information concerning the author's source. In other instances, they may be a discussion of the material or even of the

---

[16] In this chapter I am dealing largely with actual instances of narratorial voice, in the form of intrusive comments. Narrative point of view is a phenomenon that goes far beyond the unmediated voice of the narrator, and I deal with other aspects of this phenomenon in some other chapters. For example, a disparity between a character's words and actions may serve as an important indicator of narrative perspective (see, for example, my Chapters I and X). Indeed, the very fact of devoting a good deal of space to a character or an action, or, conversely, of passing quickly over it, may serve as an important indication of narrative stance, to the extent that it provides or precludes reader identification and interest.

narrative process itself,[17] and they may, in the mouth of an inept narrator, have the effect of impeding rather than facilitating humor (an analogous case being the question, coming just before a joke's punch line: "Are you sure you haven't heard this before?").

These observations are confirmed by any number of fabliaux whose narrators intrude in the most conspicuous fashion. Although I limit my comments to three of them, with passing comments about another, I would contend that my remarks about the privileged or autonomous status of fabliau anecdotes are broadly applicable to the form. I am not suggesting, however, that the specific narrative strategies are typical: the genre is too diverse to admit of such generalizations.

The voice that presents *Jouglet*, a scatological composition signed by one Colin Malet, offers commentary that is comparatively routine but, in one instance, unusually revealing. The minstrel Jouglet persuades a simpleton (Robin or Robinet), who is about to marry, to gorge himself with pears and then informs him that custom forbids a bridegroom to defecate on his wedding day. That night, Robin's suffering prevents him from performing his husbandly duties; when he finally reveals the source of his problem, his bride instructs him to go to the bed where Jouglet is sleeping and to relieve himself there. At her further bidding, he does so three times on Jouglet's bed, then once in the fireplace, once in a washpail, and in the minstrel's *viele* case. The remainder of the story tells how Jouglet repeatedly befouls himself when he wakes up, then when he tries to make a fire, further when he tries to wash his hands. A final, rather nice touch to this story, which is otherwise unsullied by subtlety, is that he himself does not open his *viele* case. Rather, he arrives in town during a festival; an unruly crowd of peasants force him to sing, and preparing to do so, he asks two of them to open the case. The result is a sound beating from which, we are told, he suffers for a year.

---

[17] This category includes problems not just of closing fabliaux but also of closing episodes and divisions, of ending one part of text and beginning another. In *Le Prestre qui dist la passion*, the priest intones "Dixit Dominus Domino meo," only to have the narrator intervene to comment, "I can't find a rhyme in -o" (which is *itself* a rhyme in -o, of course). Then, he simply proceeds with the narrative, without further comment.

Throughout most of the tale, the narrator's commentary is entirely traditional and thus undistracting (e.g., Robin "molt estoit fol e estordiz," "was foolish and simple-minded," 6). Even his intrusions to comment on his own storytelling are in most cases unexceptional. For example, ostensibly conscious of the problem of length, he asks (as do the narrators of *Estormi* and a good many other fabliaux), "Why should I stretch out this story?" Although that is a common formulaic question, usually meaning little or nothing, we can provide an answer in this case: the greater length permits him to multiply the details incrementally. The humor of the story—assuming we find scatology humorous, as did medieval audiences, if we can judge by the number of texts that exploit it—depends not on the fact itself, but on the repetition, as Jouglet's every effort compounds his problems.

My commentary on the story has left a loose end: an unconsummated marriage. As that is not the subject of the fabliau, we would not be justified in discussing it, except that the narrator himself does so. Once Robin's suffering eases, he and his bride turn their attention to sexual matters, concerning which he is woefully ignorant. But as the woman, who is obviously much less ignorant than he, prepares to offer instruction, the narrator suddenly asks again (292), "Why should I make this story any longer?" and changes the subject. We might argue that incompetent sex must surely be funnier than coprophilia, but that would be an irrelevant objection; in any case, we must admit that the narrator faithfully follows the imperatives of scatological art. He is apparently concerned less about excessive length than about the distracting intrusion of material unrelated to his primary subject. He insists that he does not really care how this turns out; he is unconcerned and does not want to meddle, and Robin can either manage on his own or else do without (291-94).

The author has a most unusual method of dealing with narrative distractions: instead of constructing the work so that they simply do not occur, he explicitly calls attention to them and then announces his indifference to them. His intrusion is of interest in another way as well, for instead of undercutting the autonomy of the anecdote, as it may initially seem to do, since the narrator is able to intervene to alter it at will, it acknowledges that autonomy by positing a sequence of available events from which he will select in order to assemble his narrative. As the narrator himself remarks, sexual intercourse has little to do with his story, but his reference to what he chooses not to

include confirms its occurrence as part of a preexistent set of fictional
events. This narrator is far less intrusive than the voice we hear in
Estormi, and less systematically befuddled, but the two of them are
involved in similar narrative projects—the selection and presentation
of material—and neither hesitates to make his own voice heard when
needed or even when not.

Few fabliau narrators are as intrusive as these, but a number
come very close. For example, Henri d'Andeli, author of the *Lai
d'Aristote*, one of the so-called "courtly" fabliaux, offers a long
moralizing prologue and a number of similarly moralizing comments
throughout. Exhibiting some of the same kinds of self-consciousness,
he announces after his prologue, "Now I must return to my story"
(38); he tells us that he himself liked the story when he first heard it
(40-41), and he adds remarks related both to technique and to the
value of appropriate (i.e., morally upright) tales:

> . . . bien doit estre desploïe
> Et dite par rime et retraite
> Sans vilonie et sanz retraite,
> Quar oevre où vilonie cort
> Ne doit estre noncie à cort;
> Ne jor que vive en mon ovrer
> Ne quier vilonie conter,
> Ne ne l'empris, ne n'emprendrai;
> Ja vilain mot n'entreprendrai
> En oevre n'en dit que je face;
> Quar vilonie si defface
> Tote riens et tolt sa savor. (42-53)

That is, fabliaux should be told properly and in rhyme, without any
vilonie, because a work in which anything improper occurs should not
be presented in polite society. The narrator himself will shun
impropriety, because it is unworthy to be heard in court and because
it is aesthetically destructive.

Finally, it will be useful to return briefly to *De la dame escolliee*,
analyzed in a previous chapter but worth mentioning anew because
it dramatically demonstrates, first, that redactors play a major if not
always beneficial role in the elaboration of fabliaux, and second, that
in a good many texts the anecdote itself resists alteration from

manuscript to manuscript far better than does the commentary that accompanies it. That is a corollary to an observation made some years ago by Jean Rychner and noted in Chapter I: some fabliaux are excellent examples of one aspect of the phenomenon that eventually would come to be called *mouvance*: by specific design, and not simply as a result of the inevitable processes of manuscript transmission, redactors would sometimes modify the text of fabliaux to fit them to satisfy particular needs or publics. In *De la dame escolliee* (not studied by Rychner), there is in one version of the story a narrator whose visibility approaches that of the narrator of *Estormi*.

As I noted earlier, this violent narrative, known to most readers only through the inadequate edition of Montaiglon-Raynaud, is the cruelest of all possible mother-in-law jokes and the most uncompromisingly misogynistic of fabliaux. It will be recalled that the text involves a man who, as a lesson to his wife, "corrects" her mother's presumptuous and domineering ways by announcing that she has testicles and by surgically removing them, viciously slashing her thighs without benefit of anesthetic and then presenting palmed bull testicles as proof. These events are prefaced by a diatribe in which the narrator addresses "men who are married / and put your wives above you / so that they dominate you" and adds that "you are only bringing shame upon yourselves" (1-4). Twice he announces that he will get on with his story, and twice he resumes his diatribe, urging men not to treat their wives kindly but to punish the foolish and presumptuous creatures. Finally, after twenty-two lines, he begins, but at intervals throughout the text, as well as in the conclusion, he interrupts to offer commentary.

Here is one of the most prominent of all fabliau narrators, and we can have little doubt that he both enjoys the story and heartily endorses the corrective measures it recommends. And yet, if we examine the manuscripts of this work, instead of relying on Montaiglon-Raynaud's version, which is based primarily on MS. Paris, B.N. fonds français 19152, we find some striking modifications, not of event but of commentary. The independence of narrators vis-à-vis their material is illustrated by a comparison of the printed edition with, for example, B.N. fr. 12603 (listed but little used by

Montaiglon-Raynaud).[18] In this manuscript, the prologue, the repeated promises to begin, and the repeated interruptions that permit the narrator to reiterate his views of domineering women (by which he appears to mean women in general)—all that is simply lacking. Instead, 12603 begins with what is, in Montaiglon-Raynaud, line 25: "Once upon a time, there was a wealthy man . . . ."

At the end of the story, the printed edition praises those who punish their evil wives, curses those who are submissive to them, exhorts those who have good wives to love them but hopes that evil will befall all other women, and concludes with a remarkable demonstration of tortured misogynist logic: "Here is the moral of this fabliau: Cursed be the woman who hates men!" Contrast this to the ending of 12603, where the narrator endorses punishment for evil and domineering wives, but notes that *bonnes dames* deserve praise. He adds, "May honor come to wives who honor their husbands" and then stops, without repeating the curse on evil women and, especially, without the curious moral that concludes the Montaiglon-Raynaud edition. Whether the original version (if it is even possible to talk about an original) was the longer one, part of which was later suppressed, or instead, as seems more likely, 12603, to which a redactor added commentary, these two redactions offer two quite dissimilar impressions. Neither is a feminist manifesto, to be sure, but 12603 balances censure of evil women by praise for virtuous ones, and it avoids the obsessive, almost hysterical misogyny of the Montaiglon-Raynaud text. The anecdote itself does not differ materially from one to the other, but in 12603 the misogyny of the tale, when deprived of the corroborating force of a narrator's endorsement, is significantly weakened.

A consideration of only three or four texts does not authorize us to draw wholesale conclusions, but it may nonetheless offer some useful perceptions about the intricate interplay of author, narrator, and text, and about textual autonomy and narrative authority. The one constant element is the privileged status of the fabliau anecdote,

---

[18] Unfortunately, Noomen's editions to date do not include this text, scheduled for volume 8. Once all his volumes are completed, we will have material for an important study of manuscript variants. The importance of such variants and their potential consequences for the interpretation of a text are underlined not only in my discussion of *De la dame escolliee*, but also in some of my earlier remarks concerning *Cele qui se fist foutre sur la fosse de son mari*.

an *histoire* recognized and presented as autonomous even when, or perhaps especially when, the intrusive presence of a narrator displaces it as central focus.

The recognition of that autonomy, reinforced by truth claims (however obviously spurious) and by the persistent refusal to claim invention, refocuses our attention on authors' experimentation with commentary and narration, on their exploration of a narrator's relationship to his received material, to his craft, and to his public. The subject of many fabliaux, in other words, is as much storytelling as it is the story being told.

Conclusions similar to these have by now become routine in regard to other genres, the romance in particular, but they are anything but routine when applied to the fabliaux. Perhaps (one might object) these authors are not in fact experimenting with narrative technique; perhaps, instead of creating incompetent narrators by design, they themselves are simply incompetent. Such objections surely have some substance: in a genre that includes 100 or 150 texts, we do not have to read far to find authors who tell a bad story or tell a story badly. But there are two points to rebut these objections. First, the genre also attracted authors such as Jean Bodel, Henri d'Andeli, Jean de Condé, Rutebeuf, and a good many others whose narrators are quite visible and whose skill is beyond question.

Second, medieval authors have left us more than a few texts that turn largely or even solely on the question of narrative competence. In *Des Deux Bordeors ribauz*, for example, two *jongleurs* argue about which of them is better and has the larger repertory of literary compositions. In an effort to list all the texts they are able to present from memory, each one manages to garble every title, generally by joining parts of two different ones.[19]

If we are hesitant to credit fabliau authors with narrative self-consciousness, I suspect the problem may be, in part, that we learned

---

[19] Thus, instead of talking of Ogier le Danois and Renaut de Montauban, one of the two *bordeors* claims the ability to tell of "Ogier de Montaubant, / Si com il conquist Ardennois; / Si sai de Renaut le Danois" (49-51). He is similarly capable of recounting the adventures of the evil Gauvain and of Kay the good knight (56-57). The modern equivalent might be a boast that the speaker is an authority on the great nineteenth-century novel *Eugénie Bovary*. Incidentally, two manuscripts of the *Bordeors* diverge radically in the second half of the composition, and MR publish the variant text as a separate fabliau, entitled *La Contregengle* (see Index of Fabliaux).

Bédier's lesson too well, and while rejecting it we have not entirely forgotten it: lurking among our received ideas is the notion that the fabliaux actually *were*, as Bédier contended, uncomplicated, unadorned, unsophisticated tales intended to provide harmless diversion to bourgeois audiences. When a narrator working in another form, such as romance, intrudes or distracts, we assume design and purpose, and only as a last resort do we consider incompetence as an explanation. With the fabliaux, we most often reverse the sequence. Yet those reluctant to attribute the activity of visible fabliau narrators to compositional design must be prepared to explain how the pervasive medieval interest in language, meaning, and authority could have shaped every other literary form without touching the fabliaux.

Finally, if my conclusions belie the notion that fabliau authors could never have any purpose other than to tell a good story and produce a good laugh, they also counter the assumptions that fabliaux are, almost by definition, unencumbered by superfluities. Yet, if a fresh reading replaces those suppositions by a conviction that many authors were concerned with complex questions of narrative method and with the creation of varied narrative personas, then I suggest that our appreciation of the fabliaux has lost little and gained a good deal.[20]

---

[20] After I had prepared this manuscript for the press, a new article appeared that supports my contentions and takes some of them considerably farther: Willem Noomen, "Auteur, narrateur, récitant de fabliaux: le témoignage des prologues et des épilogues," *Cahiers de Civilisation Médiévale*, 25.4 (1992), 313-50. See in particular his comment that "Le plus souvent . . . le récit-message préexiste à la performance" (p. 315) and his observation concerning the "[d]iversité non seulement d'un fabliau à l'autre, mais à l'intérieur même de la tradition particulière d'un fabliau" (p. 349).

VIII. The Humor of the Fabliaux

Text: *Le Bouchier d'Abeville*

By Eustache d'Amiens
546 lines
Noomen, III, 237-335

[David, a butcher from Abeville, on his way home from a business trip, decides to spend the night in Bailleul. He asks lodging from a disagreeable priest and even offers to pay, but the latter refuses to lodge anyone not in orders. The butcher leaves and comes upon a flock of sheep belonging to the priest. He steals one, returns to the priest's home, and asks for lodging in exchange for a meal of mutton. The priest, not recognizing him, agrees, and they kill and skin the sheep. The priest's mistress joins them for the meal, after which they retire. The butcher then summons the priest's maidservant and, offering her the sheepskin in exchange for sex, takes her to bed. After the priest leaves the following morning, the butcher makes the same bargain with the mistress. As he then leaves the town, he stops at the church and sells the skin to the priest. Later, the two women fight over the skin, each of them arguing that it had been given to her; the priest insists instead that it is his, because he bought it. At that point, the shepherd arrives and laments the theft of his finest sheep. The priest understands that he has been the victim of multiple deceptions, but the narrator concludes by leaving to his readers the task of judging which of them deserves the sheepskin.]

Eustache d'Amiens is more specific about names, details, and geography than are most fabliau authors. The protagonist is a butcher at Abeville (Abbeville) and is named (David); the time of year is specified (the *feste Seint Martin* in Noomen's critical text, 15, but the *feste toz sains* in some other manuscripts), and we learn that he goes to the market at Oisemont (16). When he asks a woman for advice concerning lodging and refreshment, she not only makes a suggestion, but also refers to her husband by name (Mile, 47), names the priest (Gautier, 49), and tells where his wine comes from (Nojentel, 51).

In some instances, the specificity of Eustache's treatment has an evident narrative purpose. For example, the fact that the butcher found nothing to buy—the animals being too expensive and of poor quality—initially appears to be gratuitous and potentially distracting information, of the sort that may inhibit humor. Yet it is quickly justified by the statement that, having spent none of his money, he fears robbers and therefore wishes to stop for the night.

Details that are crucial include descriptions of the priest, who is described as puffed up by pride (58) and who haughtily refuses to provide lodging for any *vilein* (72). These references are the essential "set-up" for the intrigue: in the fabliaux, as elsewhere, a pompous and uncharitable priest invites his own undoing. Even at this point in the text, before any plots have been hatched or stratagems contemplated, the reader can have no doubt that the priest will be taught a lesson; the only questions can be the means and perhaps the extent of the butcher's revenge.

As I have noted earlier, the fabliaux, as a general rule, offer few genuine surprises.[1] In fact, when the butcher, learning that a flock of sheep belongs to the priest, steals one of the animals and returns to the priest's home, we not only anticipate a deception, but we begin to foresee the form it will take. Offered a meal of his own sheep, the priest promptly agrees, and Eustache tells us that the priest always coveted others' possessions (136). He adds that the priest preferred a "dead one" to four live ones, but he leaves it to us to decide whether the reference is to sheep or to people, or both.

Although Eustache is no more subtle here than he had been earlier,[2] the contrast between the priest's reactions in this encounter and in the previous one is itself subtly productive. Initially, the butcher had tried to procure lodging by appealing to the priest's sense of charity. Rebuffed, he had then offered money (81) by

---

[1] It is typical of the fabliaux not to leave us in suspense about the outcome of the story, and, as I will note later in this chapter, the few apparent surprise endings of fabliau anecdotes are most often *only* apparently a surprise.

[2] The reference to his lack of subtlety is by no means a condemnation. He is not subtle because his purpose is better accomplished without subtlety.

proposing to purchase anything the priest had to sell; that effort failed as well. We may presume that such a bargain held no appeal because it did not represent clear profit for the priest, since, by contrast, the priest promptly accepts the later bargain, in which he will gain half a fat sheep and will have to sacrifice nothing except a bed for the night. The distinction between the two scenes emphasizes, more than authorial commentary could have done, the extent of the priest's greed, and the initial portrait, of a man who rudely refuses a reasonable bargain, fairly demands revenge.

The second scene (implying that a fine meal is worth more than money) may illustrate in addition his attachment to pleasures of the flesh, a vice that afflicts the large majority of fabliau priests: they have a decided appetite for good food, copious drink, and the pleasures of intimate female company. Nor is the last of these foreign to the priest in this fabliau: we learn that he has a mistress, a revelation that Eustache offers in entirely matter-of-fact fashion. We may later be somewhat more surprised—but surely should not be—to learn that she has borne him children.

The characters dine on the priest's sheep, and the deceiver has been deceived. The story might therefore have ended at this point, but justice served is clearly not revenge accomplished, and so it does not. And here the role of the mistress comes into play. The presence of the mistress serves to emphasize first off that this meal is a special and joyous occasion: the priest, jealous as well as unpleasant, usually sends the woman away when there are guests, but tonight he invites her to dine with the two of them, as of course he must if the story is to develop as planned by the author.

The plot thickens: several manuscripts (*C*, *O*, *T*, but not Noomen's critical text) contain a line that suggests, almost in passing, either that the butcher is attracted to the mistress or, depending on the manuscript, vice versa. It does not really matter which, for the slightest suggestion of attraction offers Eustache the opportunity to continue the story, multiplying ruses and deceptions in a manner that was, to judge from the number of tales that do so, obviously appealing to medieval audiences. This text will thus dramatize not merely poetic justice, not merely revenge, but specifically revenge many times over.

The butcher's seduction of the servant is accomplished without great effort: it requires only the promise of the sheepskin and, when she expresses fear that he will tell her mistress, of his discretion. The impression is that her objections are perfunctory, a reaction unsurprising in a fabliau maid. The seduction of the mistress is initially more difficult, and she resists even when he offers her the sheepskin and money besides, as well as when he says that he will kill the priest if he surprises them together. However, the argument that finally tips the scale is virtually identical to that used successfully with the servant: the butcher promises never to tell anyone. Like many women in the fabliaux, she is inhibited not by scruples, but by fear for herself or her reputation.

The seduction scenes are not, in fact, particularly comical, but they nonetheless offer an excellent example of poetic justice taken nearly to its logical conclusion. The initial offense may seem slight (a haughty rebuff), but the punishment—loss of a sheep and of the virtue of his mistress and his maid, while the butcher also gained what he had originally requested—seems fitting rather than excessive. Part of the reason is that the priest is presented as a generally unpleasant man who, for that reason alone, merits punishment.[3] (Of course, the very fact that he *is* a priest might well be sufficient cause for deception in the fabliaux.) Yet much of the pleasure we derive from a reading of this text is purely aesthetic: the simple multiplication of deceits is appealing, and to that appeal is added the progression from the butcher's seducing the priest's maid to his seducing his mistress to deceiving the priest himself. And that is matched by the priest's progressive discovery of the ruses and his conclusion: "[David] ma mesnee m'a fotue; / Ma pel meïmes m'a vendue" ("he has laid my whole household and sold me my own sheepskin," 503-04).

Perhaps curiously, the end of the fabliau does not show the butcher going away in triumph; he has already left, we do not see him again, and the narrator himself makes no further reference to him. His disappearance lets us savor the multiple complications he has wrought. Those complications include details that further illuminate the priest. He argues with the two women, not because they slept

---

[3] Howard Helsinger writes of this fabliau: "David, the butcher of Abeville, is so clever we may forget the moral direction of his acts, although it is because his acts are moral—intended as punishment of the corrupt—that we can enjoy them without guilt." See his "Pearls in the Swill: Comic Allegory in the French Fabliaux," in *The Humor of the Fabliaux: A Collection of Critical Essays*, ed. Thomas D. Cooke and Benjamin L. Honeycutt (Columbia: University of Missouri Press, 1974), p. 105.

with the butcher, but because they dispute his claim to the sheepskin—a concern that demonstrates yet again the greed that made him originally accept the bargain offered him (a sheep in exchange for a bed for the night).

He asserts that neither of the women will have the sheepskin unless an impartial judge awards it to one of them. Thereupon, Eustache asks the audience to decide the matter. In fact, that is a question without an answer, for if any of them deserves it, they all do—or, more accurately, none of them does. Eustache's concluding request is not, as it purports to be, an actual request for a judgment, but an affirmation that the situation is a stalemate; and the lack of resolution removes our attention from their argument and refocuses it on the humor of the butcher's successful ruses.

*

The subjects of comedy and humor are far too vast and too complex to be considered thoroughly in this or any single essay. The point I have emphasized repeatedly, concerning the impossibility of making wholesale generalizations about the fabliaux, is applicable with particular force to the question of humor: these are too complex and disparate a group of texts to admit of a specific kind or theory of comedy. Our inherited assumptions about fabliau art would suggest that comedy of action predominates, but we have seen in this volume a number of instances, and there are a good many others, in which humor is generated by linguistic means. In addition, we could adduce examples of a *comédie de moeurs* (for example, in the manners and mannerisms of priests, peasants, merchants, or women), and in at least a few cases we could justifiably talk even about comedy of character.[4]

Thus, at best, we can generalize about the humor of a certain group of fabliaux, or we can analyze and describe the methods exploited by a particular author to elicit laughter from the audience of a particular tale. But it is clearly impossible to talk about *the*

---

[4] Nor should we forget that, as I suggested in Chapter II, a number of texts that might be considered fabliaux are (by intent) largely without humor. The present chapter is thus not intended to account for all fabliaux, but certainly it is true that humor is the purpose of the vast majority of them.

principle or principles underlying fabliau humor in general; and our discussions must respect that impossibility.[5] Were we to try to be exhaustive in such an enterprise, we would surely produce a discussion either so general or so fragmented as to be entirely vain; we would also identify a good number of methods that produce decidedly unhumorous texts. Nonetheless, if we limit ourselves to larger groups of texts and keep in mind the dangers of generalization, we can profitably identify certain tendencies, certain methods that clearly appealed to a good many fabliau authors and audiences.[6]

The first and largest group is obvious enough to be predictable and therefore banal: fabliau authors and audiences had a decided taste for erotic tales.[7] Nykrog reminds us (p. 55) that, of the 147 texts he counts as fabliaux, 106 exploit erotic themes. Within this group, it is by no means surprising, though it is somewhat more useful, to note the frequency and obvious popularity of works that ally

---

[5] Related to the methods by which humor is created are techniques that *permit* that creation. For example, a good many authors of fabliaux go to some lengths to show the husband, say, as cruel, stupid, or naive, thus avoiding audience sympathy for him. In hearing or reading *Le Vilain de Bailleul*, we most likely consider than any man as irremediably stupid as the husband richly deserves to be cuckolded. However, such a traditional distancing device is in most cases unnecessary, and the simple announcement that we are about to hear a fabliau is normally sufficient: an audience expecting to hear a fabliau would know what to anticipate and would normally suspend traditional responses of sympathy or censure.

This conclusion must, however, be qualified, for sensitivity to humor at the expense of women or married women or priests—or conceivably of cuckolds—has the power to bridge that distance and provoke, not direct sympathy for the character, but disapproval of the entire process of telling and hearing humorous stories about women and others.

[6] It surely goes without saying that I will not be talking about why we laugh at fabliaux—that is a matter for psychologists rather than literary scholars—but only about which elements of fabliau texts recur frequently in contexts devised to provoke laughter.

[7] Most often, in such situations, a man is seducing a woman; in some cases, such as *La Borgoise d'Orliens*, the woman takes the initiative. And in a good many instances (represented by *L'Esquiriel*), the seduction is mutual; that is, there is not a victor and a victim, but rather a collaborative linguistic and sexual project.

sex with deceit.[8] Moreover, a great many of the fabliaux that modern tastes (and apparently medieval ones as well) consider to be among the best examples of the form use deceit either for purposes of seduction or to permit illicit sexuality by concealing it from the woman's husband. Works like *Les Braies au cordelier*, *La Borgoise d'Orliens*, *Auberee*, *Cele qui se fist foutre sur la fosse de son mari*, *La Pucele qui voloit voler*, and a good number of others fall into this category; but the category is so broad as to be of limited value, for no two of these fabliaux accomplish sexual relations by precisely the same ruse. In addition, there are numerous permutations of this pattern; for example, *Le Bouchier d'Abeville*, as indicated in my analysis, uses seduction for the purpose of deceit (or revenge), rather than deceit for seduction. In other words, as I have insisted frequently, categories and generalizations are a necessary evil: when talking about some 150 texts we inevitably categorize them, but to understand their art and their humor we would have to examine them individually.

If it is difficult to accept that the fabliaux had a moral purpose or function,[9] it is nonetheless true that an impressive number of them depict retributive justice or justified revenge. We have seen instances, such as *La Pucele qui voloit voler*, in which a presumptuous woman is "put in her place" or (as in *La Borgoise d'Orliens* and *Le Bouchier d'Abeville*) a jealous husband or a crudely selfish person may be punished. *Brunain* dramatizes a system of justice in which God, nature, or accident avenges the wrong done to the poor by an acquisitive priest. *Le Sentier battu* juxtaposes symmetrical insults, one that humiliates a man, the other, the quick-witted man's answer, that humiliates the woman who had ridiculed him.

An additional characteristic of fabliau humor is the authors' and audiences' decided taste for the multiplication of deceptions or the multiplication of effects provoked by a single cause. This preference frequently leads fabliau authors to offer an elegantly complex grouping of incidents designed to produce a desired result, itself humorous, out of a single cause or course of events. Thus, to take

---

[8] Ménard, however, points out (p. 137) that the ruse is emphasized far more than the sexual relations themselves.

[9] But see my discussion of morals, in Chapter IX.

revenge for a single affront, it does not suffice for the Butcher of Abeville to steal the sheep, or even to steal it and trade it for a meal and bed: he must also seduce the priest's servant, seduce his wife, and then sell the skin to its own owner.

   Narrative multiplications explain part of the interest of *Gombert et les deus clers*, a setting of the cradle motif[10] that doubles the basic intrigue: two clerics seduce a man's wife and daughter, and then, through a process of mistaken identity, one of them recounts the events to the man himself. *Les Quatre Sohais Saint Martin* is the ultimate multiplication, with genitals sprouting out of control over the protagonists' bodies. In *Jouglet*, Robin defecates not once but four times, taking quadruple revenge on the deceiver. *Estormi*, *Les Trois Boçus*, and *Barat et Haimet* offer multiple murders, thefts, and deceptions. In *La Borgoise d'Orliens*, it is not enough to deceive the husband; the woman has him beaten as well, and in addition she arranges it so that he is delighted to be abused. *Le Jugement des cons* has three young women in turn judge whether they are older or younger than their vaginas.

The preceding remarks are, however, descriptive rather than analytic; they refer to groups of themes and categories of texts. They thereby offer little insight into the mechanisms that actually permit and produce humor. To accomplish that, we need to look not at, but *within*, fabliaux. There, we are likely to settle first on the notion of ambiguity, on the *effets de dissonance* noted by Ménard, or on the kind of disjunctive composition that consistently keeps characters at cross-purposes, most often preventing them from communicating and understanding properly.

We can go one step farther in our analysis. A careful reading of many fabliaux suggests that authors play frequently on the logic linking cause to effect, sometimes frustrating our expectations but more often confirming what we know (or should have known) had we grasped or shared the logic of the text itself. The key is that, although the textual logic may be unconventional, it is in most cases internally consistent, and it is sufficiently crucial in the production of fabliau humor to merit some detailed discussion.

Any reference to the logic of these texts may be immediately suspect, because, as my previous discussions have emphasized

---

[10] See Chaucer's *Miller's Tale*, for example.

repeatedly, the fabliaux do not generally function according to the "rules" of our world. They frequently develop outlandish plots: corpses returning repeatedly to "haunt" someone, a wife able to persuade her husband that he is dead, a claim (apparently given credence) that a woman was impregnated by a snowflake, a magic ring that produces instant and enduring erections, a guessing game using smell and taste to identify excrement. And there are the ubiquitous genitalia: detachable genitals, lost and found genitals, talking genitals, and—less frequently—normal genitals.[11] A simple description of fabliau plots might in other words suggest that the genre systematically dispenses with realism and with logical consistency in order to indulge in flights of narrative fantasy.

That suggestion is seriously misleading, however: the majority of the fabliaux do not by any means dispense with logic *or* with consistency. Instead, they construct a fictional universe in which events obey the imperatives of a logic that we happen not to share. Fantasy they may frequently be, but, at least in this instance, fantasy and logic are in no way mutually exclusive; the fabliaux *are* logical constructs, and their logic is invariably related to their humor and often the key to it.

Neil Schaeffer, in *The Art of Laughter*, suggests that "laughter results from an incongruity presented in a ludicrous context."[12] He is doubtless correct, but his contention tells us little until we have defined and refined the notion of incongruity. In the fabliaux, the incongruity is less often internal than external; that is, it is a disparity between expectation and event or, more precisely, between our logic and that of the text. One of our essential tasks in considering the humor of the fabliaux must be to define their textual logic and the interplay, for comic effect, of that logic with our own. Such a project will permit us to move beyond an inventory of often superficial thematic similarities and differences. When Nykrog categorized fabliaux as erotic vs. nonerotic, then as triangle situations vs. other

---

[11] On the subject of sex organs with "a life force of their own," "having their own power and existence," see Thomas D. Cooke, "Pornography and the Comic Spirit," in *The Humor of the Fabliaux: A Collection of Critical Essays*, ed. Thomas D. Cooke and Benjamin L. Honeycutt (Columbia: University of Missouri Press, 1974), p. 141.

[12] (New York: Columbia University Press, 1981), p. 17.

erotic texts, and so on, he provided a convenient classification, but that does not tell us much about the internal comic mechanism of fabliaux.[13] We need instead to identify the functional relationships that are independent of subject matter or tone. We need to consider less what they are about than how they work, and such investigations will necessarily concentrate at least as much on the nature of fabliau language and logic as on the choice and development of incident.

Jokes, as I have suggested earlier, are close modern relatives of many fabliaux, and we might profitably begin there. Schaeffer (*The Art of Laughter*, p. 45) relates a traditional joke concerning an attractive woman who passes a construction site. All the workers except one whistle and make predictable remarks. When the silent one is asked why he did not participate, he explains that this is his day off. In this joke the humor, such as it is, derives not from an unexpected event but from an unexpected *explanation* of event, that is, from a small shift in logic, similar to shifts we will identify in a good many fabliaux. While we may assume that lechery is part of the construction worker's *character*, the joke posits it instead as part of his *duties*; it goes with the job, but not quite in the way we assume. Laughter results from the transference from one logical system to another, from the substitution of one premise for another, or, in more traditional but less precise terms, from surprise or frustration of expectations. In the case of this joke, the specific surprise here is that we had not anticipated the discrepancy between its premises and our own.

Once again, humor resides less in the event, which is at best mildly amusing, than in the explanation or logical basis for it. To demonstrate that fact, we could keep all the elements of the joke but remove the humor merely by establishing its premise in advance, to wit: one of the normal duties of a construction worker is to whistle at attractive women, and, consequently, the man who is off duty does not necessarily do so. The joke clearly loses something unless we are allowed to retain our own premises for a time before finding them suddenly supplanted by those of the text.

Functionally, a number of fabliaux are closely related to this joke. For example, we might think again of *Le Vilain Asnier*, in which the peasant ass-driver, accustomed to the smell of manure, faints while

---

[13] *The Fabliaux* (Copenhagen: Munksgaard, 1957), esp. Chapter II.

making a detour though the spice market. The humor derives from the fact that the text (a study in cultural relativity if ever there was one) dramatizes a premise that departs from our ordinary assumptions about nature. Whether spices are to be preferred to excrement is clearly a question of conditioning, habit, and, at least in this text, class identity. I would contend that this work functions in virtually the same way as the construction-worker joke. Its elaboration is perfectly consonant with its logic; to the extent that comedy is invariably linked to an incongruous event or development, the incongruity has far less to do with the character of the *asnier* than with the presuppositions we bring to the text.[14]

One conclusion to be drawn from a study of the fabliaux may be suggested at this point: whether dealing with medieval or with modern comic texts, we need to refine considerably the notion and role of surprise. I have previously contended, in disagreement with Thomas Cooke, that surprises are not often the key to the fabliaux.[15] More precisely, much of their humor arises not out of genuine surprise endings, which I consider rare, but rather out of *apparent* surprises, by which I mean resolutions that may be unexpected, but *only* if we do not carefully and properly follow the logical development of the poem; that is, if we do not anticipate the divergence of the work's logic from ours.

We tend to bring to our reading of a text a traditional notion of logic—an empirical logic, as it were—which may or may not be shared by some of the characters. But the fabliaux tend in many instances to develop their own internal, or narrative logic, which diverges from ours in some way; many authors of fabliaux exploit that divergence to produce the essential comedy of their works. In other words, the author plays on the perceptual habits that lead us to assume that

---

[14] Similarly, *La Crote*, which I discussed very briefly in my introduction, is (mildly) humorous because we expect the husband to find excrement disgusting, whereas he is instead delighted at his ability to identify it by taste. A certain ambiguity is inherent in his actions: the taste of excrement ordinarily would be found repulsive, the success in a contest exhilarating. The two views—both of them logical and natural—cannot be held simultaneously by a fabliau character, and the narrator creates humor by having his character ignore the reaction we expect.

[15] In my review of his *The Old French and Chaucerian Fabliaux*. See *Res Publica Litterarum*, 2 (1979), 368-69.

logic *dictates* a particular result of a particular preparation. To the extent that they do contain surprises, they are due to our abrupt realization not only that our expectations will not be met, but also (and especially) that the outcome of the work was prepared according to a perfectly consistent logic that we simply happen not to have shared or initially perceived. Humor results as much from the second realization as from the first. We are hoist with the petard of our own presuppositions; we "bite" on a fabliau no less than on a riddle.

As the preceding remarks imply, the bases of the fabliaux are very often ambiguous, involving puns, plays on words, the literal use of figurative language, statements and actions susceptible of misinterpretation, and so on. As deconstructionists have taught us, *all* language is ambiguous by its nature; it is "inescapably figurative; in other words, no word or phrase really means what it literally seems to mean and, in fact, the figurative meaning or meanings of the words deny their literal sense."[16] While this statement offers a useful insight (especially into the questions of metaphor and euphemism discussed in my chapter on language), we need to extend the concept of ambiguity far beyond the basic idea of coexistence of figurative and literal meanings. In the fabliaux, we are dealing with a genre that posits, at least by implication, the basic ambiguity of life and experience, as well as of language. We may thus encounter not only two or more meanings for a word or expression, but also two or more potential explanations for a fact (e.g., *Le Vilain Asnier*) and two or more plausible motives for an act.

A number of fabliaux, constituting the primary group of texts to be considered here, exploit systematically the discrepancy between literal and figurative meanings. In *La Vielle qui oint la palme au chevalier*, for example, the simple woman does not properly understand the reference to greasing someone's palm in order to obtain a favor. She performs that action literally, using *du lard*. Fortunately, the recipient of the grease is amused by her naiveté and grants her request, thereby realizing (against our expectations) the prediction that she would profit from greasing his palm. Similarly, in *Brunain la vache au prestre*, an avaricious priest tells a couple that whatever they give will be returned doubly. We are witness to their

---

[16] Ellen K. Coughlin, "Discontent with Deconstruction and Other Critical Conditions," *The Chronicle of Higher Education*, 17 February 1982, p. 21.

apparent stupidity when they give the priest their cow, Brunain. Again, however, we find a transfer from the figurative to the literal level, and the promise of profit is kept when Brunain returns home leading the priest's cow.

These examples relate incidents that "backfire" on those who attempt to take advantage of simple or naive people. The way a child cuts through linguistic subterfuge—or, rather, the process by which he unwittingly reveals such subterfuge by mistaking figurative for literal language—is illustrated by *Celui qui bota la pierre*. In that work, a woman's priest-lover threatens to take her to bed ("je vos foutré," 24) if she kicks a stone by her door. She invites his sexual attentions by kicking the rock. When her husband later returns home, their small child warns the man that if he kicks the stone, "our priest will fuck you just as he did my mother" ("nostre prestres vos foutra ja, / Sicom il fist ore ma mere," 46-48).

A particular example of linguistic confusion, in which the distinction is not between literal and figurative but between two literal but ambiguous uses of language, is provided by *Estula*, which offers a related situation: a man who hears sounds in his garden thinks they are made by his dog and calls out to him: "Estula." But "Estula," which conveniently happens to be the dog's name, also happens to mean something else: "Are you there?" The thief hiding in the garden dutifully answers: "Yes, I'm here." He responds to a meaning not intended by the speaker but perfectly reasonable and coherent—and an unequivocal illustration of the essential ambiguity of logical and linguistic systems in the fabliaux.

A fabliau that functions in a somewhat similar way, but with one important refinement, is *Le Vilain de Bailluel*, discussed earlier. In this text, it will be recalled, a man returns home and complains that he is dying from hunger. Never one, apparently, to let a golden opportunity pass, his wife takes his figurative language literally—not, in this case, through naiveté, but through craft and design. But then she succeeds in imposing her literalistic interpretation on him, persuading him he *is* in fact dead. She lays him out on a bed and sends for a priest on whom she has had designs for some time. She takes the priest to bed, and the husband watches, furious but, since he is dead, powerless to interfere. He is caught not only by his stupidity but, more to the point, by the logic of the story.

In all these cases, and in a good many others, the poem is animated by the interplay of literal and figurative meanings.[17] Yet, as my earlier remarks implied, this interplay appears actually to be a local variation, one form of a larger pattern involving the coexistence of discrete systems of logic within individual texts. In such cases, which include in one fashion or another the majority of fabliaux, the humor of the text derives precisely from the discrepancy between two kinds of logic: the one we innocently bring to it and the one that functions, in a quite consistent if eccentric way, within it.

For example, in *La Vielle qui oint la palme* and *Brunain*, the author plays cleverly on the *reader's* understanding of figurative language: *we* have knowledge denied to the rather simple characters. Yet that knowledge is used against us, for comic purposes, when the figurative proves to be the functional level of the text. If we are surprised, it is not that logic is subverted, but rather that the logic we bring to he work is supplanted by another kind, peculiar to the text.

It is essential to note that the logical system of the text is not only eccentric, but also internally consistent and coherent. The source of the comedy, in my view, is double: it is both the consistency of that logic and its divergence from ours. In *Le Vilain de Bailluel*, for example, either the man is eminently stupid or the situation is absurd (or both), but "absurd," in this instance, means only that it does not obey the rules of what we would call "the real world." In the fabliau world, however, such a correspondence is clearly not required. Once the text establishes the discrepancy between our premises (those of everyday or empirical logic) and those of the work itself, the progression of the events is unassailably logical: it is proper that the man, being dead, be laid out on a bed; as is customary at such a time, a priest is called; and it is self-evident that a corpse cannot speak or move.

There are a good number of fabliaux that, in terms of tone or subject matter, appear to have nothing in common with those already discussed, but that nonetheless function in much the same way. An illustration of this "functional" relationship of dissimilar texts is offered by *De la dame escolliee*. While the tone and character of this text contrast strikingly with those of the fabliaux already discussed in

---

[17] As Howard Helsinger reminds us, St. Paul warned that "literal-mindedness is not only foolish, but also . . . fatal." See his "Pearls in the Swill," p. 94.

this chapter, its technique and construction offer little more than a permutation of the pattern we have already analyzed.

De la dame escolliee is unlike *Estula* or *Brunain* only in that the interplay of language and understanding is here dependent, as it had been in the *Vilain de Bailluel*, on a character's conscious choice. Although we are told that the mother finally believed she had testicles (516-17), that belief is not really essential: the work is so constructed that belief and disbelief are irrelevant. The point is that once the existence of her testicles is posited, whether literally or only figuratively (as with the expression "wearing the pants"), it generates an effective logical development, supplying both the pretext and the means for punishing her. And since any repetition of her behavior may be imputed to the same cause, it may be expected to result in additional emasculation. As in the fabliaux alluded to earlier, figurative language is transferred to the literal level; but in this case, the transfer occurs because the husband consciously chooses and enforces it. That is, once he adopts a literal explanation for her problem, that literalness provides the remaining plot elements. Here, it is not a question of mistaking figurative for literal, but rather of an intentional substitution that serves one character's ends. But the essential point is that once the substitution is made, the work follows in an entirely logical fashion on the basis of the new premise thereby established.

There are several other fabliaux in which the intrigue is based on a character's decision to transform an "illogical" premise into a logical one. An instructive example is *L'Enfant qui fu remis au soleil*. A man returns home after a two-year absence to find his wife with a new baby; this development clearly calls for an explanation, and hers is that she swallowed a snowflake and it grew into a child. While we may receive her explanation with some skepticism, the husband appears, surprisingly, to accept it unquestioningly. His apparent gullibility is explained when, a full fifteen years later, the man takes his son to Italy and sells him into slavery, afterward informing his wife that the hot Italian sun melted their child.

This is an amusing example of revenge (with the child an unfortunate pawn), in which one lie is met by another, equally absurd. But the key to the humor is the fact that the second lie is an entirely logical extension of the first. Once the husband pretends to believe her, she has no choice but to believe him: she is caught in a trap of her own setting, and again, the humor is due in equal measure to the internal consistency of the narrative logic and to the discrepancy between that logic and ours. Here, however, there is an additional twist, as we eventually learn that the discrepancy is itself illusory and the husband no more gullible than we.

The fabliaux discussed thus far are all relatively simple compositions, built on a single plot or anecdote. Certainly, comic technique is far more obvious and more easily studied in such texts, and the analysis becomes increasingly difficult as we move away from simple jokes or rejoinders, toward extended intrigues, especially those involving parody. A particular problem is posed, for example, by fabliaux that depend for their humor on "courtoisie du vilain" or on the establishment of a courtly sub- or superstructure.[18] The author may derive a comic effect from the deflation of courtly pretensions; or, in a few cases, the comedy is instead the result of an overlay of courtly logic on an initially noncourtly situation. In either case, the establishment of a logic based on courtly principles is one of the most complex developments of the fabliau genre; yet, here again, the comedy ultimately springs from the discrepancy between the texts' apparent and actual logic.

In *Cele qui se fist foutre sur la fosse de son mari*, analyzed in the introductory chapter, we noted an example of the intrusion of an uncourtly logic into a courtly one. We would not ordinarily expect a grieving widow to accept a blatant seduction attempt. Something happens in this work that we may not have foreseen. But, in fact, we should have foreseen it, for, as we saw, the work offers us ample cues about the insincerity of the widow's grief. Had we initially noted and properly interpreted the cues, this work would contain no surprises; because we likely missed them, we do not grasp until late the fact that the squire and the lady are out of the same mold.[19] He does not, as it may at first appear, deceive her in spite of her grief and her courtliness; rather, he offers her a welcome opportunity to follow her

---

[18] See above, my discussions in chapters I and, especially, IV.

[19] For the sake of the present argument, I am oversimplifying the problem. As I will point out again in the next chapter (and have already suggested in Chapter I), we should not dismiss out of hand the notion that the widow was deceived. Instead, her complicity in her own seduction is all the more humorous because it is overlaid on the *apparent* victimization of a poor grieving widow.

inclinations and shed her pretenses of courtliness and socially acceptable conduct. We have been privileged observers, but probably not very astute ones; otherwise, we would have understood much earlier that her acquiescence is the logical conclusion of a development begun much earlier.

This pattern inverted, that is, an overlay of *courtoisie* on a situation that is initially courtly only in terms of its setting, is the basis for *Guillaume au faucon*. After the wife has repelled Guillaume's many advances and even threatened to denounce him, it doubtless comes as something of a surprise that she eventually relents and accepts his love. The surprise is still the result of our inability to follow the cues or to read the text according to its own logic, but in this case we may not be entirely at fault: the cues were in most cases withheld from us until we are told at the end that she has come to love Guillaume.

This work embodies certain traditional courtly premises, implied but not explicitly developed. Had we not been denied access to the developing textual logic of the work, we would have seen that the composition is essentially courtly. The central question, reflecting the theme of numerous courtly texts, is whether Guillaume's proposition is frivolous or, conversely, whether he is willing to risk personal danger for her sake. In its outlines, the text develops in traditional courtly fashion: he confesses his love, she resists and tests him, he persists and proves his willingness to run any risk, and she eventually yields once the genuineness of his love is demonstrated. The reversal in the plot is a perfectly logical consequence of her newborn love for Guillaume, but since the birth of that love is not explicitly shared with us, her explanation of Guillaume's fast may come as a surprise.

The novel development in this work is the author's withholding of one logical pattern from us, but both are nonetheless present. It may be that the humor, uncharacteristically, derives in large part from our surprise—the cues are lacking—but the surprise is due not to an abridgment of logical development, but simply to our realization that the work has shifted from one logical pattern to another. Moreover, the comedy depends here not only on the divergence of two logical lines, but from their subsequent re-convergence as well. When the woman concocts an explanation (the falcon) intended to protect Guillaume, her husband concurs with her plan and becomes her accomplice. He plays Pandarus to his wife and his servant, by directing her, in effect, to give the young man what he wants.

I have examined only a few fabliaux in this chapter, and it would be presumptuous to conclude that the observations made here will invariably hold for other texts. As I have stated repeatedly, virtually any observations we may make about the fabliaux are, at very best, applicable to the majority of them, but certainly not to all. Some fabliaux are no more than very simple anecdotes or puns (although we should again recognize that, by their nature, puns fully exploit linguistic ambiguity); others are portraits or character studies, while others still are complex and sophisticated parodies. A certain number of them may not conform, at least not precisely, to the principles outlined here. But, on the other hand, the fabliau that produces a genuine surprise ending by contradicting its own narrative premises is rare indeed, if not nonexistent.

In concluding, we may return to Schaeffer's view of laughter, as resulting from "an incongruity presented in a ludicrous context." As I suggested, his contention is acceptable because it is very general, but for that very reason it tells us little. What is essential is to locate and identify that incongruity and to define its nature. The fabliaux rarely or never offer an incongruity between preparation of *plot* and resolution of plot, but rather between preparation of *reader* and resolution of plot. The fabliau author most often bases his method on the coexistence of dual systems of logic, and humor is born the moment there is a transfer from one system to the other, or the moment it becomes apparent that an expected transfer cannot take place. The reader may be a privileged observer, but never *simply* an observer; in fact, one of the important keys to the comedic success of the fabliaux is the ability of many of their authors to engage our complicity, usually unwitting, in the creation of humorous effect.

IX. Closure

Text: *Des trois dames qui trouverent un vit*

118, 128 lines[1]
MR, IV, 128-32; MR, V, 32-36

[Three women on a journey find a large penis on the ground. There ensues a quarrel about which woman will keep it. To settle the argument, they go to a nearby convent to ask the advice of the abbess. The latter examines the object with considerable interest and announces that it is the recently lost bolt from the convent door and that she will therefore keep it. The women, displeased to have their property confiscated, swear never again to solve disputes in that manner; rather, she who finds such an object will keep it and treasure it as a valuable relic, of the sort honored by all women.]

Montaiglon-Raynaud edited two manuscripts of this text as two different fabliaux, although they are obviously variant versions of the same narrative. The intrigue is virtually identical in the two, but some details and particularly the concluding narratorial statement are different. In the shorter version (the 118 lines of MR IV), the women are traveling to Mont-Saint-Michel on a pilgrimage they had promised to undertake—a wise course of action, according to the narrator (9). One day, specifically at the hour of tierce, they discover a penis in their path.

I have sometimes encountered readers who have assumed that what the women find is a dildo, but there is no reason to think so. First off, were that what it was, it would be typical of fabliau authors to say so. Moreover, the notion of "autonomous" genitals is hardly foreign to the fabliaux. Genitals may exist apart from a person, as

---

[1] The two figures represent the two versions of this fabliau: MR IV has 118 lines; MR V has 128. Unless otherwise indicated, my observations refer to the version in MR IV.

here, or they may be thought to do so, as when the naive husband of *La Sorisete des estopes* believes his deceitful wife's statement that she had left her vagina at her mother's home. (The husband later mistakes a mouse for the vagina.[2]) Jehan Bodel's *Le Sohait des vez* tells of a dream concerning a *marché aux vits*. Elsewhere, genitals may talk in *Le Chevalier qui fist parler les cons* or multiply in *Les Quatre Sohais Saint Martin*.[3] Clearly, a review of fabliau conventions gives us no reason to doubt that the women found exactly what the narrator says they found.

In addition, the humor of this text depends to a considerable degree on the fact that this object is found during the course of a pilgrimage, submitted to an abbess for arbitration, and referred to as a relic. The humor of the story might not be lost entirely, but surely it would be diminished, were this object no more than a replica of a *vit*. And, finally, any lingering doubt is resolved by the text given in MR V (from MS. Paris, B.N. fr. 1593), where, we are told, they found a very large penis along with two testicles (13-14). (The narrator in that manuscript, perhaps to fill out the line and facilitate the rhyme with *gros*, adds a curious and very specific detail: it is a penis without any bones, "où il n'ot point d'os," 14.)

---

[2] On this fabliau, see the discussion by Ora Avni, in *The Resistance of Reference* (Baltimore: Johns Hopkins University Press, 1990), pp. 2-14.

[3] R. Howard Bloch, in *The Scandal of the Fabliaux* (Chicago: University of Chicago Press, 1986), esp. ch. 2, relates such characteristics to castration. While the association may be *literally* correct—simply by definition, because sex organs are separated from a body—I am not persuaded that such separation has the implications Bloch sees in them. I do agree with Bloch that the "detached body [is] a sign of the detached nature of signs" (p. 67), but otherwise, and perhaps simplistically, I read into these tales nothing more than an objectification of genitalia for purposes of sexual humor. That is an emphasis hardly foreign either to modern "off-color" jokes or to medieval fabliaux; even when firmly and conventionally attached (cf. *Le Fevre de Creil*), sex organs share with copulation pride of place (as it were) as one of the most popular emphases in humorous narrative. If there is a profounder significance, it escapes me.

On the other hand, there is a clear connection between this organic disjunction or dislocation and other kinds of disjunction in fabliau texts: between preparation and conclusion, between our assumptions and a character's logic (see Chapter VIII), between word and deed. Perhaps it belabors the obvious to point out that humor, whether in medieval fabliaux or modern jokes, depends inevitably on disjunctions.

The woman who finds it is delighted, "for she knew what it was" (19). The second woman demands her share, but the finder denies the claim, and an argument ensues. Curiously, although the title and the second line announced a fabliau concerning three women, the third is immediately forgotten; she neither demands part of this prize nor speaks of anything else. She is simply forgotten, a fact that reflects not the negligence of the narrator but a common characteristic of many fabliaux: while certain fabliaux carefully tie up all loose ends (cf. *Le Bouchier d'Abeville*), others choose to ignore inessential matters. The three women of the title may be simply a number imposed by tradition, as in a fabliau bearing a similar title, *Des trois dames qui trouverent l'anel* (cf. also *Les trois aveugles de Compiegne*, *Des trois meschines*, *Des trois boçus*, and others). Whatever the reason for her initial presence, she is a dispensable narrative commodity and as such is simply ignored.

Suggesting that the argument be settled by an abbess, the second woman points out the convent, notes that it is a holy place, and says that those who are there serve God night and day (41-43). She gives assurances that the abbess will offer a true and proper judgment, and they agree to accept that judgment. Seeking the abbess, they are told that she is hearing Mass and that they must wait. This retarding element in the story is another narratively gratuitous detail, but similar delays are common in fabliaux: in a genre known for rapid and economical action, a great deal of time is spent waiting, whether by lovers anticipating a rendezvous (*Le Chevalier qui recovra l'amour de sa dame*, *Auberee*, *La Borgoise d'Orliens*), by husbands whose wives are enjoying a dalliance elsewhere (*Des trois dames qui trouverent l'anel*), or by other characters awaiting an opportunity or a propitious moment. In addition, the abbess's attendance at Mass emphasizes her piety and contributes further to the humor of the less-than-devout interest she will show in the penis.

When the problem is explained to her, the abbess declines to dispense justice in the abstract but insists on examining the evidence. Once it is placed before her, the narrator notes (85-88) that she scrutinizes it closely; we are then told for emphasis that "the abbess looked at it willingly" and that she sighs long and "granz suspirs" before rendering her judgment. Not surprisingly, given such reactions, her decision is that the penis will be confiscated, but the objectification of genitals is carried very nearly to its logical conclusion when she contends that it is in fact the bolt for the door.

This explanation is interesting in two ways, in addition to being both an ingeniously humorous reaction and an example of what I called the objectification of genitals. First, the image of "the bolt on the abbess's door" to designate genitals is a metaphor not unlike those in a number of other fabliaux, where the penis is presented, for example, as a colt protected by two guards and the vagina as a fountain in a meadow (*La damoisele qui ne pooit oïr parler de foutre*). Not only does the abbess's invention force a resolution of the dispute, but the euphemism suggests the particular use she may have for the object, with her "door" secured by this promising "bolt."

Second, and this is a point to be made about a good many fabliaux, this sequence contains an indeterminate element, by which I mean a question the answer to which is both uncertain and ultimately irrelevant. Some readers may well ask whether the women could really have believed that the penis was a bolt for a door. Surely (such readers will object) these women could not be so naive. And, in fact, both versions of the fabliau tell us that the finder of the object, if not the other women, *did* know what it was (IV, 128, l. 19; V, 32, l. 17).

Much of the humor of the anecdote turns, in fact, precisely on the predicament the women have created for themselves, when their selfishness leads them to submit their dispute to an outside party for mediation. The point is simply that, once the women have agreed to accept the judgment of the abbess ("she will judge truly"), they have no choice but to do so; and if her decision is to keep the item, they are bound by it and have no recourse, however absurd may be her identification of the object.

This is, I believe, a perfectly satisfactory answer to possible questions one might raise about the presumed naiveté of the women: whether they actually believed her or could *possibly* have believed her. Yet there is a much more crucial consideration to be raised here, and that is simply that such questions, or at least attempts to answer them, are to a considerable extent misplaced in most readings of fabliaux.

That brings us, albeit belatedly, to one of the fundamental "rules" of reading fabliaux: there are certain questions that are either precluded by the conventions of the genre or that must be left without answer. This principle ought to be so self-evident that it does not require rehearsal, although both pedagogical experiences and some critical readings of fabliaux suggest the contrary. Simply put, the fabliau cosmos is the creature of a highly selective literary consciousness. Although the fabliaux, like most other medieval literary forms, are a thoroughly conventionalized set of texts, one of their conventions is the freedom claimed by the author and narrator to choose the questions that may not be asked and those that must remain unresolved.

Prominent among the former, the inappropriate matters, is the desire to know how one can fail to recognize a person one knows well; yet a number of fabliaux turn on just such a failure. Only rarely is there any attempt to rationalize this failing; one case in which such an attempt is made is *Du Chevalier qui fist sa fame confesse*, in which we learn that the woman's illness has dimmed her senses and prevents her from recognizing her husband. In other instances, such as *La Borgoise d'Orliens*, there is no explanation beyond the information that the event occurs at night. It is hardly less remarkable that, after initially, even repeatedly, failing to recognize a person, a character eventually "looks carefully" and only then recognizes that person.[4]

Characters may fail to recognize not only a familiar face, but also a familiar voice (as in *Berengier au lonc cul*). A husband may mistake a strange man's voice for that of his wife (*Barat et Haimet*). A woman may copulate with a stranger and assume that he is her husband (*Gombert et les deus clers*), or a man may, even in daylight, see every detail of his wife's body except her face and yet not recognize her (*Les Deus Changeors*).

Yet, ultimately, questions about such failures are largely irrelevant, because the emphasis is not on *whether* one would be likely to recognize a friend or spouse, but on the humorous possibilities offered if one does not. Mistaken identities are a frequent source of humor, and, as in the joke, the fabliau finds it sufficient simply to

---

[4] Of course, this motif is not limited to fabliaux. In the *Mort Artu*, for example, Arthur talks at length with his sister Morgan and fails to recognize her until she identifies herself. Then he looks closely and knows it is she. The fabliaux, however, use the motif extensively and effectively for comic purposes. See Jean Frappier, ed., *La Mort le Roi Artu* (Geneva: Droz, 1964), p. 60.

stipulate them. They must happen as they do because the joke depends on it.

The fabliaux posit a cosmos in which our customary rules of logic and perception can be either suspended at the whim of the narrator or, conversely, observed rigorously, should the narrator's purposes require it. Pragmatic conventions (concerning the usual rules of logic, the usual way the world works, the normal understanding of what is possible and what is expected) give way to conventions of the genre itself. We are thrown into the world of the joke, where realism is most often entirely irrelevant. Fabliau characters are bound by generic conventions as surely as these women are bound by their decision to submit judgment to the abbess.

If the fabliaux prohibit some questions, they permit others in situations where it is important that they remain without response. Fundamentally "undecidable" elements occur frequently, as for example in *De la dame escolliee*. In that text, we do not know whether the wife actually believes what is said of her mother: that she had testicles. (We *are* told, as I noted earlier, that the mother herself finally believed it.) But for the daughter—and this is the central point—it hardly matters what she believes, since she cannot escape the threat of physical violence. She will be chastened through fright if she believes her mother had testicles, and she will be equally chastened, but through intimidation, if she understands the reference to testicles as a metaphor, as a thinly veiled threat of mutilation. She has no way out of her dilemma, but the reader is led by either of two possible interpretations to a common conclusion.

At the risk of belaboring a particular text, I would like to return once more to *Cele qui se fist foutre sur la fosse de son mari*, which is a more complicated case. Again, between two divergent paths to a single conclusion, the text may initially appear to invite us to make a choice: was the widow tricked, or was she the equal of the squire in trickery and in lascivious behavior? It is difficult to accept that she really wants to die (at least by the time the squire arrives) and, especially, that she believes in the fatal effects of sexual intercourse. As we saw in chapter I, the textual logic of this fabliau differs slightly from manuscript to manuscript, but the critical point is that, whatever our reading of the widow's grief, the "joke" works, either as an illustration of the squire's talent for seduction through deceit or as tacit complicity between a lascivious widow and the squire who offered her a welcome opportunity. Although there is strong and, to my mind, persuasive textual support for the latter explanation, the effectiveness of the composition is lost if, having made our interpretive choice, we assume that the rejected alternative was simply wrong from the outset. The intriguing question is whether her grief was assuaged *by* the squire or before his arrival, and the complexity, subtlety, and humor of this fabliau depend on the initial coexistence of two possible readings and the way one emerges gradually to displace and supplant the other.[5]

But whether such questions receive tentative answers or remain completely open, it is crucial for us to recognize the existence of multiple explanations and to respect the ambiguity of many fabliau texts. Readers, at least modern ones, are inclined and trained to assume that, of multiple possible readings, one is correct and others must be rejected. But it would be a misreading to reject as invalid a choice that the author has left open; it would ultimately impoverish the text. Such a rejection would not affect the conclusion of the action, but it would artificially resolve the enigma that is part of the work's complexity and, therefore, of its appeal.

Berengier au long cul offers a similar enigma. In that text, it is surely inappropriate to wonder whether the husband realizes that the "knight" who humiliates him is his own wife in disguise, much less to wonder at his failure to recognize the wife's posterior and genitals as those of a woman. The text does not tell us that he ever understands clearly how he has been undone, and we cannot draw that conclusion. In fact, the fabliaux typically tell us everything we need to know, and often more, and when information is withheld, we should respect that silence. The narrator does *not* tell us, for example, that at the later mention of "Berangier au long cul," the husband suddenly realizes that he had cowered before his own wife; the author thus respects the enigma and presumably expects us to do so as well. But if the specific *answer* to such questions may not matter, I am persuaded that the

---

[5] It is revealing to note that, were it *impossible* for us initially to assume naiveté on the widow's part, the fabliau would be reduced to a simple and quite crude anecdote: the widow quickly forgets her grief and thus eagerly accepts the sexual attentions of the first man who passes. The story might be shocking, but not very amusing. The humor comes from our gradual shift from assuming one premise to accepting another.

comic value of the text derives in part from the ambiguity of the situation, that is, from the fact that such questions persist. Thus, whether or not the husband ever knows that his adversary was his wife, or even a woman, he clearly comes to understands the critical fact: that he has been caught in a lie and a ridiculous masquerade, that his cowardice is now known, and that he no longer has any influence over his wife, who is henceforth free to indulge her every whim and satisfy her every desire.

*

The conclusion of *Des trois dames qui trouverent un vit* tells us that when the dispute concerning the lost-and-found item is settled (to the satisfaction of no one except the abbess), the women curse her and affirm that never again will they ask for such a decision; instead, the one who finds something will keep it all. Thus, the experience has had didactic value for the women. They have learned from it, and what they have learned is not unlike the implied lesson of *Le Couvoiteus et l'envieus*: the person who wants too much for himself and who wants another to have nothing ends up by losing everything.[6]

The narrator underlines his lesson on the effect of selfishness by emphasizing not only the women's resolve, but the value of what was lost: henceforth, the finder of *tiele chose* (113; meaning, presumably, any object of value, although the passage could also be taken specifically as a reference to a penis) will keep it forever as a precious relic honored by all women. Here is an interesting twist. The reference to a relic emphasizes both the value of the object and the religious associations provided by the nuns and abbey; yet the abbess claimed the penis not as a relic but as an ordinary, utilitarian object (for which she had a very specific use in mind).

There is no explicit moral, nor is one needed. The anecdote, which is both humorous and ostensibly instructive, has been completed, and the cruel lesson has been learned by the women and, simultaneously, by us. The narrator thus has no need to provide any conclusion other than the summary of that lesson. Consequently, the

---

[6] I note that the lesson is "implied," because the author of this fabliau does not append the expected moral to the text. The point is, however, entirely clear.

lines that refer to the women's resolve to keep such an object as a relic (115-18) are also the final words of the fabliau.

Or rather, they are the final words of one version of the fabliau (MR IV, 128-32, entitled *Des .III. dames*), and, in considering the various ways fabliaux end, it is useful to look also at the ending of the other version, or, more precisely, another manuscript of the text: MR V, 32-36. There, once the abbess has made her decision, the women leave, and the narrator adds a rambling conclusion of almost thirty lines (101-28). That conclusion refers to the abbess as a *tricheresse* (a devious or deceitful woman) and adds the observation that judges are like her: they are covetous, and the poor will never receive fair treatment from them. There follows a moral, to the effect that one should without hesitation share one's findings with others:

> Par essample vos mostre et preuve
> Que se nul de vos avoir treuve,
> S'il i a compaing ne compaigne,
> N'atende pas que il s'en plaigne,
> Mès rende l'en toute sa part.

("By this exemplum, I demonstrate that if any one of you finds something of value and has a friend, he should not wait for that friend to claim it, but should give him his portion," 117-21)

Added to that moral is a proverbial pronouncement: "Cil se repent trop tart, / Qui se repent quant a perdu" ("he who repents after he has lost repents too late," 122-23). The narrator then explains that proverb—such a person has waited too long (124)—and, adding a second proverb, says he wants us to understand that "L'en pert bien par trop atendre" (126), meaning roughly that "he who hesitates is lost." Then a third conclusion and a third proverb: "Mès en la fin di en apert: / Cil qui tot covoite, tout pert" ("In closing I say clearly: he who wants everything loses everything," 127-28).

Readers may conclude that this narrator simply does not know when to stop. The proverbs are generally appropriate to the subject, even though it is unclear that three proverbs are more effective than one; but the generalization about judges is clearly irrelevant to the humorous intent, and only barely logical. More to the point, the reader who wends his way through the conclusion(s) will find that the slightly malicious humor of the anecdote has been diluted or lost. Obviously, the other version of this fabliau, with nothing added to blunt the narrative effect, is superior.

Or is it? To modern tastes, to those for whom the anecdote and its humor are the heart, the epitome of a fabliau, to those for whom the introduction and conclusion of a fabliau should frame and emphasize the anecdote and otherwise remain transparent and/or invisible, the second variant of *Des .III. dames* undeniably is less effective. I admit that those tastes are also mine. But, individual tastes aside, we must take fabliaux on their own terms and attempt to evaluate medieval assumptions as well as our own. It is by no means obvious that a good many authors, narrators, and medieval readers would agree that morals, even inappropriate ones, and digressions are out of place in fabliaux.

*

Closural problems are fascinating in the fabliaux. Evidence, in the form of unfinished or carelessly terminated texts (including the romances on which authors might be expected to have lavished considerable attention), suggests that medieval writers were not overly concerned with closural methods and that it often sufficed to note that "the story ends here" and stop writing.

Yet, in a genre like the fabliau, where the humor of the anecdote could theoretically be undermined by an awkward or digressive conclusion, we may be surprised that the endings of fabliaux do not exhibit more uniformity, especially in terms of their brevity or conventional moral conclusions. It may appear, as in the diatribe against lawyers, noted above, that some fabliau authors had a good deal of difficulty closing their texts, that, like the one discussed above, they simply did not know how to end. Or, if we want to make this same point positively rather than negatively, we may observe that, to judge from the variety of closural methods, varying even from one manuscript to the other of a particular fabliau, the conventions of the genre offered and even encouraged a good deal of freedom for commentary that we might characterize, in recent times, as "extra-diegetic."

In only a few cases does the anecdote of a fabliau fill the textual "space" within which it is framed.[7] In other fabliaux, space remains, and it is generally far greater, and the methods more diverse, at the end than at the beginning. That is, the very first line of a fabliau may introduce the intrigue, and when it does not, the introductory lines are usually very few. Authors most often introduce their fabliaux simply if not gracefully, with the formulaic "I want to tell you a fabliau" or even "once upon a time." In some instances, they offer an indication of what is to be illustrated in the text. Digressions and moral reflections do occur at the beginnings of fabliaux, but lengthy introductions are comparatively unusual, at least in contrast to the extended commentary that often closes these texts.[8] The reason is obvious: to grasp and retain the audience's interest, the narrator can afford to delay only minimally before proceeding to the anecdote. Once the story is told, there are few impediments to the narrator's indulging his taste for commentary or digression.

Clearly, then, the conventions and narrative demands of the genre did not impose strictures on endings as much as on beginnings. Once the anecdote is concluded, the author/narrator obviously considered himself free, within broad limits, to end the text when and how he wished. With endings, while there are generally accepted formulaic

---

[7] In practice, there are almost always a few words of introduction and conclusion. Among the fabliaux that best illustrate the near-coincidence of anecdote with text are Noomen's second version of *La Damoisele qui ne pooit oïr parler de foutre* (IV, p. 84), which begins "En iceste fable novele / Vos conte d'une damoisele . . ." ("In this new fable I tell of a young woman," 1-2), and *La Borgoise d'Orliens*, beginning with a two-line question ("Would you like to hear the courtly story of a *bourjoise*?") before launching into the story, after which the author concludes with a two-line summary and a one-line moral ("Il meïmes brasça son boivre!," "he brewed his own drink," 325).

[8] Some of the exceptions to this practice are startling for the length of the introductory material. Besides the commentary in one redaction of *De la dame escolliee* (already discussed), examples include *La Fole Larguece*, whose author, "Phelippes," begins with a long moralizing statement including a proverb; it is only in lines 40-41 that he indicates his intention to "commenchier un conte," but before launching into the story he adds another brief moral that has proverbial force: "qui sueffre aucune fois mesaise / il set mius puis conjoïr l'aise" ("he who once experiences discomfort is better able to enjoy comfort thereafter," 43-44). That is followed by the narrator's command to his audience to listen and not interrupt, and the story finally begins on line 47.

conclusions available to the author, none—not even the traditional moral that closes many fabliaux—imposes itself with the force that underlies the simple need to provide a straightforward and undistracting beginning.

One manuscript (Z) of *Les Quatre Sohais Saint Martin* illustrates this freedom and also confirms yet again a major point made in my chapter on narrators. That manuscript offers the same moral as the critical text, noted above, but it then adds more than fifty lines of misogynistic reflections on Solomon (whose wisdom was not great enough to prevent him from being betrayed by a woman), on Samson, Constantine, and Hippocrates. Clearly, the anecdote's conclusion affords the narrator or redactor a good deal of latitude to indulge in reflections or diatribes.

To talk of freedom in ending is not by any means to suggest that the fabliaux are simply exempt from closural conventions; it does, however, imply that those conventions are far from restrictive. The possibilities are multiple: the narrator can simply announce that the story is ended, or he can simply stop, with no comment at all, once the anecdote is concluded; he can interject commentary on the very general subject of the text, relating that subject in some cases to his own situation; he can append a suitable moral or an absurd semblance of a moral. The first of these approaches is in fact less common than we might expect, conditioned as we are to assume that the paramount virtues of fabliau narration are economy and brevity. Rather, a surprising number of fabliaux or, as noted in regard to *Les Quatre Sohais Saint Martin*, manuscripts of fabliaux give evidence of a decided resistance to closure.

In the category of free commentary we can list the discussion of judges in the fabliau just analyzed, as well as the lengthy diatribes that close MS. Z of *Les Quatre Sohais Saint Martin*, one redaction of *De la dame escolliee*, and a good many other fabliaux. Rutebeuf's *Le Pet au vilain* offers reflections on the poor lot of *vilains*: excluded both from heaven, because a *vilain* should not be in the presence of Our Lord, and from hell, by the event recounted in the text, they are outcasts who are left to "chanteir avec les reinnes" (70) or do penance in the land of Cocuce.[9] The bitter tone, the sympathy for those on the fringes of society, and the reference to the author in the

---

[9] See discussion of this text in Chapter VI.

third person all contribute to the construction of Rutebeuf's persona[10] at the same time as it draws the text to a close by widening the focus from the protagonist to the plight of his class.

Estormi, too, provides moralizing reflections at the end, but the running commentary throughout is so pervasive that it would make the closure unexceptional, were it not that the author, in his mania for commentary, adds a full series of morals. First, he offers a reflection that has the force of a moral when he says of the fourth priest, ". . . teus compere le forfet / Qui n'i a pas mort deservie" ("many an innocent man pays for crime," 586-87).[11] Only a few lines later we encounter the first explicit moral: "Par les prestres vous vueil aprendre / Que folie est de covoitier / Autrui fame ne acointier" ("by these priests I want to teach you that it is foolish to covet another man's wife," 592-94). Next, we learn that priests should take care not to drink from the same cup as those "Qui par lor fol sens ocis furent" ("who died for their stupidity," 610). Finally, the author instructs us "Mes on ne doit pas . . . / Avoir por nule povreté / Son petit parent en viuté, / S'il n'est ou trahitres ou lerres . . ." ("one should not revile a relative because of his poverty, provided he is not a traitor or thief," 620-23).

Clearly, this narrator relishes his role as teacher as much as his pose (if that is what it was) as a bumbling storyteller. His four moral pronouncements condemn lascivious priests, as the narrative would indicate, but they also comment on the unjust suffering of innocent men and commiserate with those who, owing to their poverty, are reviled by their relatives. The diversity of these reflections blunts the effect of any one of them, but that is entirely in keeping with the generally inept stance of this narrator.

In *Estormi* we saw that the effect of narrative commentary and digressions was to remove our attention from the anecdote and refocus it on a point or a plane outside it. We experience narrating activity rather than narrative. The same can be said of "extra-

---

[10] The subject of Rutebeuf's persona is admirably treated by Nancy Freeman Regalado, *Poetic Patterns in Rutebeuf: A Study* (New Haven: Yale University Press, 1970), esp. ch. 5.

[11] Noomen has these words spoken by Jehan, but they sound less like his sentiments than like an authorial reflection.

diegetic" material, whether in the form of free commentary or morals, that *follows* the anecdote. Not only does it serve as a closural device, ironically signaling the end of the text even as it prolongs it, but it moreover emphasizes the performative nature of fabliau narration—we are no longer "in" the story, but are talking or hearing *about* it. Furthermore, the absence of such commentary or its seamless integration into the anecdote, though praiseworthy to a modern sensibility that seeks and values unity, effaces the signs of the narrator's controlling presence and thus, I would suggest, blurs one of the defining features of fabliaux. Whether a fabliau impresses itself on our memory may depend on its comic structure, its outrageousness, or another feature; whether we retain an impression of its *narrator* depends instead on what happens outside the story, which often means after the anecdote ends.

That brings us directly to the question of the morals that close many fabliaux. This has traditionally been a vexing problem for fabliau scholars. Most have agreed that they are evidence of the descent of the fabliaux from, or their relation to, fables; but there has been little agreement about the way we should read them. Many are perfectly logical conclusions of the narratives to which they are appended, but a great many others are not. Some exhibit a rather twisted logic, and some are pure absurdities without discernible links to the anecdote. Indeed, a good many fabliaux offer the semblance of a moral that is, in fact, only a restatement of the lesson of *that* text; for example, the reader who knows the fabliaux reasonably well will doubtless anticipate a condemnation of women to follow *De la dame qui se venja du chevalier*, but the conclusion tells us instead only that "trop fu *ceste* fame deable" ("*This* woman was very diabolical," 270, my emphasis).[12]

Armine Kotin suggests that the fabliaux had morals because the Middle Ages could not conceive of "events or characters as not

---

[12] Beyer suggests that many fabliau morals are not universal reflections of moral truths but merely "retrospective commentary" on the specific story that has been told. See Jürgen Beyer, "The Morality of the Amoral," in *The Humor of the Fabliaux: A Collection of Critical Essays*, ed. Thomas D. Cooke and Benjamin L. Honeycutt (Columbia: University of Missouri Press, 1974), p. 40.

having a meaning beyond the literal."[13] Yet, although the medieval mania for moralizing cannot be denied, I find it impossible to imagine that medieval people, on an ordinary day, were unable to enjoy a good story or a good joke without assessing its moral implications. Even some fabliaux themselves refer to the simple enjoyment of a good story, without moral: for example, *Boivin de Provins*, 369-76, has a magistrate hear about an event and enjoy it so much that he has it told repeatedly to his family and friends, who similarly appreciate it and laugh about it; there is no reference to their drawing a moral conclusion.

Moreover, *De la dame qui se venja du chevalier* (MR VI, 24) divides fabliaux into two varieties, *essemples* and *risées*, and thus establishes, or at least contends, that some fabliaux are designed to produce nothing more than entertainment and laughter:

> Vos qui fableaus volez oïr,
> Peine metez à retenir;
> Volentiers les devez aprendre,
> Les plusors por essample prendre,
> Et les plusours por les risées
> Qui de meintes gens sont amées.

("You who wish to hear fabliaux should take care not to forget them. You should be eager to learn them, in some cases to derive a lesson from them, and in others because of the humor that many people enjoy in them," 1-6)

Insofar as we can judge from the character of the stories themselves, a good many of the fabliaux that offer moralized reflections are actually of the *risée* variety, meaning that the moral is either irrelevant or an actual element of the humor.[14] It may well be

---

[13] Armine Avakian Kotin, *The Narrative Imagination: Comic Tales by Philippe de Vigneulles* (Lexington: University of Kentucky Press, 1977), p. 10.

[14] See on the subject of fabliau morals (and of the moral content of the body of fabliaux) Howard Helsinger, "Pearls in the Swill: Comic Allegory in the French Fabliaux," in *The Humor of the Fabliaux: A Collection of Critical Essays*, ed. Thomas D. Cooke and Benjamin L. Honeycutt (Columbia: University of Missouri Press, 1974), pp. 93-105. He contends that the fabliaux are in some way "moral"; for example, he

correct that "the strength of the medieval tradition of moralized tales was so strong that even a highly 'immoral' tale required a moral ending" (Kotin, p. 10) or at least—and this is a crucial difference—a *pseudo-moral* ending. Yet it is unlikely that medieval audiences would be blind to the potential for irony in a form that appended a moralizing statement to an anecdote in which, at least for the modern reader and doubtless for the medieval audience as well, no moral purpose can be discerned. If the opening lines of *La Borgoise d'Orliens* can, with cutting irony, describe as "very courtly" the story of a woman who arranges to have her husband brutally beaten in one part of the house while she is enjoying a dalliance with her lover in another room, we must entertain the possibility that the morals appended to certain texts may be similarly ironic.

It is often the case that a moral or a proverb directly contradicts the logic of the anecdote. For example, *Le Chevalier a la robe vermeille* concerns a man who refuses to trust his own eyes and is therefore deceived by a woman; yet the moral says a man should never believe his own eyes and should believe his wife rather than himself. This, as Schenck points out (p. 30), is a "blatantly sarcastic" conclusion, and even if we did not accept her assumption about authorial intent, it is obvious that a moral that contradicts audience expectations will possess some degree of ironic value.

Similarly, in *Le Fevre de Creil* a man who fears that his wife might be attracted to another man tempts her by mentioning the man's physical endowment; the wife yields to temptation and is on the point of committing adultery when the husband intervenes. Several morals are possible. We might expect the narrator to conclude that the man who does not trust his wife will find his mistrust justified; or alternatively, knowing the misogynistic bias of many fabliau narrators, we might anticipate a generalization about women's tendency toward lascivious behavior. Perhaps we might even expect an endorsement of the husband's action: he who does not trust a woman is prudent

---

notes (p. 103) that corrupt characters are often punished (see above, Chapter VIII, n. 3). He does not, however, deal with the peculiar problems attending texts in which adultery goes unpunished. Even there, it is often true that the cuckolded husband is old or cruel or stupid, but those characteristics tend to be reported routinely, as if they are merely traditional traits rather than an effort to emphasize the morality of their cuckolding.

to test her. Instead, and perhaps incredibly, the narrator praises the husband's wisdom, noting that the man was wise, not to test her, but instead to intervene at the last minute. If this moral is not simply to be disregarded, that is, if it has any impact at all, it may be humorous: a man who mistrusts his wife and tests her fidelity must be ready to intervene to prevent the very behavior he feared. Suspicion of women is thus a self-fulfilling prophecy.

Les Trois Boçus has a double or triple moral, at least part of which is thoroughly inappropriate and illogical. The narrator first tells us, ". . . onques Dieus ne fist meschine / C'on ne puist por deniers avoir" ("God never made a young woman who could not be had for money," 286-87); this may be at least partially logical, in that the woman had married a rich hunchback—but that is not the point of the story. Then, the second part of the moral adds, "Nor did God ever make anything else that could not be had for money" (288-91); that is entirely illogical. Finally, we are told, incomprehensibly, "shame on the man who values money too much" (294-95), a defensible notion that has absolutely no connection to the story. How are we to take that moral? Either the audience saw a connection that escapes us, or the audience saw no connection but did not require one, or—and I think this most likely—the audience found humor in the absurdity of such a gratuitous moral. That is, I am persuaded that the illogic of some morals is not in fact a "problem," but is instead a crucial ingredient of the work's humor.

Although some morals are, for whatever reason, illogical conclusions, *Le Pescheor de pont seur Saine* offers an example of a moral that is the perfectly logical reflection on a text that is itself absurd. To test his wife's contention that her love for him is not dependent on sex, a man tells her that his penis has been cut off, and as proof he presents the penis of a drowned priest. His wife immediately loses interest in him, and that situation persists until he eventually informs her that God has reattached the organ. The moral is, strictly speaking, an entirely logical lesson—a man is a fool who believes a woman, for women want only sex—but we cannot imagine that any reader could assume that the purpose of this particular narrative is to prepare for a moral teaching.

Finally, we have some instances in which the moral implied, often with great clarity, by the anecdote simply never materializes.[15] For example, the story of *Le Couvoiteus et l'envieus* raises every expectation that the moral will concern the "duper twice duped" (e.g., "He who through jealousy seeks the suffering of others will suffer more in turn"). But, in fact, the text remains silent on the meaning of the story, which lacks that or any other moral.

Morals are a selective feature of fabliaux. As I noted in my chapter on fabliau women, a good many fabliaux present male and female characters of equal greed or stupidity, only to criticize the woman in a moral. Neither of the characters in *Les Quatre Sohais Saint Martin*, for example, is above serious reproach; yet the narrator ignores the husband's foolish and wasteful wish and simply condemns that man "Qui mieux croit sa femme que lui" ("who believes [or trusts] his wife more than himself," 199).

We should note in passing that this moral is identical, almost word for word, to that of *Le Vilain de Bailluel*, indicating that fabliau authors shared not only sentiments but also proverbs or proverbial observations, movable conclusions that may be a significant aspect of fabliau performance. That is, there may well have been a store of stock fabliau conclusions, some of them moralized, others simply standard formulaic endings—from which the author could choose one that fit or, if his intent dictated, one that did not, confident in either case that the audience would recognize and appreciate the moral.

Contrary to Kotin's notion that fabliaux must have morals because the fundamental character of medieval literature is moralizing, we must conclude that authors were free to add a moral or not; if they chose to, it could make sense or not; if it did not, it could represent either an inversion or a perversion of textual logic; and if he wished, the author could multiply morals.

Whatever the case, it is obvious that morals, logical or not, appropriate or not, are fundamentally a closural device in the

---

[15] That is, sometimes it does not materialize at all, but in other instances there is a moral that diverges sharply, in nature or in degree, from what we anticipate. An example of the latter is *La Veuve*; see my comments (Chapter II) on its conclusion.

fabliaux.[16] Given this extraordinary freedom to use, misuse, double, or omit morals, to express personal concerns or voice social criticism, or simply to finish the text at the same time as the joke, we should hardly be surprised by the extraordinary range of concluding methodologies. Almost anything goes, apparently, but the creative choices authors make as they close their texts surely cannot be dismissed as meaningless expressions of the medieval mania for moralizing or as the residue of a traditional form. The ends of these texts contribute fully as much as the beginnings and middles to the complexity and complexion of fabliaux.

---

[16] This is not to deny the traditional assumption that fabliau morals are the vestigial remains of the morals that served as an essential component of apologues. That explanation concerns origins; my present point concerns function. The two are in no way mutually exclusive. On this subject, see Beyer, pp. 22-23.

X. Conclusion

Text: *Les Perdrix*

156 lines
Noomen, IV, 1-12

[A man who has killed two partridges asks his wife to prepare them for dinner, and he invites the village priest to share them. The woman cooks them, then tastes them, finally devours all of them. To escape punishment, she leads her husband to believe the birds are ready for eating, and she sends him to sharpen his knife in order to carve them. When the priest arrives, she informs him that her husband intends to castrate him. The frightened priest runs away, whereupon the woman tells her husband that the fleeing man has stolen the partridges. The husband chases the priest, shouting a warning that he is "taking them away warm," but that he "will leave them here" if he is caught. The priest escapes, and the moral is that women are deceivers by nature.]

The story of the partridges is frequently anthologized and well known, and detailed commentary is probably unnecessary. It can, however, serve as a useful point of departure for some concluding comments on the fabliaux.

Roy J. Pearcy has suggested that "fabliau plots evolve in the shadow of uncertainty and misapprehension which falls between perception of the data of sense experience and the knowledge of external reality those data are supposed to generate, through proper interpretation, in the mind of the perceiver."[1] He goes on to explain that, routinely in the fabliaux, one character proffers to another character "a complex of sense data either ambiguous in itself or rendered so by the context of the exchange between them" (p. 68). Indeed, a second look back at most, if not all, of the fabliaux

---

[1] "Investigations into the Principles of Fabliau Structure," in *Versions of Medieval Comedy*, ed. Paul G. Ruggiers (Norman: University of Oklahoma Press, 1977), p. 68.

examined in this volume will confirm the validity and importance of this insight.[2]

In a more general sense, we may say that the fabliaux and related texts typically offer an account of the initial disruption and eventual reestablishment of a narrative equilibrium. Their initial situation is static, which in this instance may describe a *potentially* disruptive situation, such as a woman who has a regular lover, provided that situation is not yet known to another character. The body of the fabliau presents the disruption of this situation by (for example) a seduction, the discovery of a lover, an accidental murder, the desire for material gain, or, in the case of *Les Perdrix*, the wife's irresistible temptation to eat the partridges; the conclusion of the fabliau ordinarily restores it. The distance separating reality from perception, or one character's perception from another's, may be a crucial aspect of the upsetting situation, as in *Brunain* or *Le Vilain de Bailluel*, but we should recognize that this irony is more often the instrumentality by which the crisis is resolved, as in *Le Bouchier d'Abeville*, *La Borgoise d'Orliens*, *De la dame escolliee*, *Les Perdrix*, and others.

A number of additional points should be made about the gap separating phenomena from the perception of them. One is that authors of fabliaux, like tellers of jokes, may unapologetically manipulate a situation to provide the necessary conditions for humorous occurrences. They may thus choose to impose conventions of misunderstanding to meet the narrative demands of fabliaux. For example, as indicated in my previous chapter, a good many characters curiously fail to recognize the voice, the body and sex organs, even the face of their spouses; then, when the story requires it, they "look more closely" and recognize the person. This question falls into the category of those one is not supposed to ask: we are expected simply to grant that what the narrator says is correct, for no other reason than that he has said so.

The category of narrative manipulation (a word I use without negative connotations) includes the overdetermination of some

---

[2] As I suggested earlier, though, we need to be careful in generalizing about the anti-prudery fabliaux. They use language that, technically speaking, is ambiguous, because it *could* and usually does mean something other than what the words ordinarily denote. However, it is clear and unambiguous to the principals and generally misunderstood only when overheard by a third person.

situations, that is, the imposition of an artificial selectivity that rewards fabliau strategies with the desired result. In other words, where an action might logically produce a number of results, it *happens* that one of them propitiously occurs to the exclusion of others. I have no desire to make this sound more complex than it is: it is a basic rule of the farce, the fabliau, and the joke, that the narrator/teller makes things happen as they do, sometimes artificially, simply because he *must* do so if the story is to succeed. A convention of hearing jokes or reading fabliaux not only requires us to suspend disbelief but also prohibits us from questioning the premises proposed by the narrator.

The ambiguity of *Les Perdrix* is verbal—the husband's reference to partridges is misunderstood as a threat of castration—but that verbal ambiguity depends on a physical or visual one, the husband's sharpening the knife either, as he thinks, to carve the partridges or, as the priest believes, to carve the latter's anatomy. But, unlike many fabliaux, this one offers ambiguities that are not simple misunderstandings, and they are not accidents. They are the consequence of design, by the wife in collusion with the narrator. She sets up the conclusion by fabricating a story for her husband, by having him sharpen the knife, then by telling the priest that her husband was going to castrate him, finally by telling her husband that the priest had stolen the birds. She controls *almost* every element of the situation, and the joke is dependent on her manipulating the situation so as to create the ambiguity. She has conceived an elaborate plan, comparable in its intricacy to the sequence of deceptions executed by the Butcher of Abeville.

But as ingenious as the woman is, there is an additional element that she cannot control—an element of apparent chance—and that involves the words her husband will shout at the priest. When the husband is told that the priest has stolen the cooked partridges, there are any number of epithets or threats he might logically have shouted to the priest. For example, it would have been just as logical for the husband to shout something unambiguous, such as "Bring back my partridges!" But then, of course, there would have been no joke. It is instead crucial that the priest not learn that he is accused of stealing the birds. While we may derive some satisfaction from the wife's intricate plan, the humor of the fabliau actually turns as well on the divergence between the intent of the husband and the flawed comprehension of the priest; the husband, in other words, *had* to shout something ambiguous, and the wife cannot manipulate that. Fortunately, the narrator can, and at this point he steps in to assist. In other words, the element of chance in this and all fabliaux is only *apparently* a matter of chance. A regular property of fabliau narration is the narrator's unabashed and sometimes overt manipulation of event and detail.

Auberee is among the fabliaux that will produce, out of a number of possible reactions to a situation, precisely the one required for the successful conclusion of the work. Auberee, intent on arranging a tryst between a lovesick young man and the young wife of another man, proceeds by planting the seeds of doubt about the wife's fidelity. We might expect the suspicious husband, reacting to that doubt, to quarrel with his wife or, far more likely, administer a beating to enforce her fidelity and obedience. Alternatively, he might respond by making his wife virtually a prisoner in her own home. Yet a beating will simply not work, and close surveillance is the precise opposite of what *must* happen: Auberee's plan depends entirely on an assumption that the husband will eject his wife from the house, and so he does. Without such conventional selectivity, there can be no fabliau. In the fabliaux, assumptions often function as imperatives.

A good many fabliaux rely on the same kind, if often a lesser degree, of narrative manipulation. In *La Sorisete des estopes*, for example, once the naive husband is persuaded that his wife's vagina is in the basket he is carrying, it "just happens" that there is a mouse in the basket, and his failure to distinguish a mouse from a vagina confirms, in his dim mind, his wife's story. When the man in *Estula* mistakes a thief in his garden for his dog and called the latter, it "just happens" that his dog is named "Estula," and it further "happens" that that name also means something else, that it possesses an ambiguity attributable to apparent accident, which is to say, to authorial manipulation.

In works like *Les Perdrix*, we are dealing with an obvious narrative collaboration: the character arranges what can be arranged, and the narrator takes care of the rest. If the wife of *Les Perdrix* does all her work efficiently, the narrator will see to it that her husband shouts an ambiguous threat—instead of the unambiguous ones that he might have uttered, thereby spoiling the joke—and that he specifically shouts words that the priest can construe as a chilling physical threat. In a good many other fabliaux, this collaboration may be less apparent, because the characters do not have to "set up" chains of events as did Auberee or the woman who devoured the partridges, but it is no less real. In some texts, as we have seen, certain things "just happen," simply because they *must* happen if the story is to succeed as humorous anecdote. Thus, overdetermination—narrative intrusion and manipulation—is essential, and it is frequently a positive feature of the tale, rather than a flaw. In the world of the joke, narrative manipulation is normal and expected, and often, in fact, it is the key to the humor of the story. The conventions of the form stipulate that narrative intervention is acceptable not only to provide commentary but, where necessary, to order the material in such a way as to produce the desired result.

The extent of such manipulation may be illustrated by imagining how often a casual retelling of many fabliaux might well repeat precisely this formula: "It so happened that . . . ." It so happened that there was a hole in the door (*Le Prestre qui abevete*); it so happened that the husband returned home unexpectedly (in a good many fabliaux); it so happened that a squire passed by at just that moment (*Cele qui se fist foutre*); it so happened that the dog was named "Estula"; it so happened that the butcher came across a herd of sheep belonging to the loathsome priest, etc.

In other words, as we should expect in this kind of composition, that is, in the fabliau as in a joke, there is no narrative space in which events can be allowed to develop other than as they do. There are no narrative accidents in the fabliaux. Traditionally, we assume that in "good" narrative texts, the intrigue arises naturally out of character or personal conflict, but the author has set the stage and often arranged the furnishings on that stage, in the novel no less than in the fabliau. The difference is that the conventions of the genre do not require the fabliau narrator to maintain, as must the narrators of many traditional novels, the fiction of narrative choices.

Part of the pleasure of the fabliau text may in fact be derived from the fact that in these highly conventionalized narratives everything is set up in advance, to the point that we can generally predict when complications will occur, and we often know just what those complications will be. The most obvious and perhaps most frequent instance is the woman's intention to welcome her lover after her husband leaves (generally for business). In that situation, we can be reasonably confident that the husband will return home, and we can also assume with some confidence that the woman (if not the lover) will escape punishment. This is one of a great many motifs and structures shared by two, three, or more fabliaux; not only is this sharing an inevitable characteristic of a form that partakes heavily of the humor of oral tradition, but it is an essential element of that humor. There is pleasure in the surprise punch-line of a joke, but there is a different, and perhaps richer, satisfaction to be taken from one's ability to anticipate developments. Or perhaps it is most accurate to contend, as I did earlier, that the particular pleasure derived from fabliaux is often related to the unexpected way a predictable and usually anticipated conclusion is reached.

Having discussed the endings of fabliaux, we may reasonably conclude by offering a few words about the space *beyond* the ending, or what we may assume about the future of these texts. Most often, the answer is, nothing: there is nothing at all implicit in the conclusions of fabliaux. That is, assumptions about what will happen outside of textual boundaries are generally unwarranted and illegitimate. In one of the common conclusions of fabliaux, as we have seen, the wife is chastened, sometimes physically, and vows never again to doubt her husband, and we must assume that she does not. Forever after the end of the text, the same thing occurs day after day, which is to say that, narratively, *nothing* else can happen, and the woman remains always the properly obedient, pliant wife.

In some instances, a fabliau leaves an unresolved situation that might lead us to anticipate subsequent action, were it not that the conventions of the genre ordinarily preclude it. The narrative world ends at the limits of the text. The conclusion of *Les Perdrix*, for example, fails to resolve an important part of the action: the husband still assumes that the priest has stolen the birds, while the priest still considers himself threatened by the knife-wielding husband. Yet we cannot suppose that the husband will later attempt to exact a price for the presumed theft of the birds. (Nor can we suppose the opposite.) The explanation is that the conflict between husband and priest is subsidiary to the central problem of the fabliau: the woman's need to evade punishment for her gluttony. She succeeds, and the second conflict is the solution to the first. As such, it does not itself require resolution, and the story simply ends. We can make no assumptions and ask no questions about what will happen later.

A related but more dramatic example is offered, again, by *Auberee*. In that text, the young man is hopelessly in love with a woman ("Amours l'a feru de son dart!," "Love struck him with its arrow,"58), but once he has enjoyed her sexual favors (gained through deceit, threats, and a measure of force[3]), his love for her is either forgotten or rendered irrelevant. As in *Les Perdrix*, the selective focus of the fabliau establishes its priorities and ignores secondary considerations. The "point" of this work is the intricacy and success of Auberee's plan to get the young woman out of her husband's house and into the lover's bed, then back into the house and into the good graces of the now-happy cuckold. In a way that some readers may find unsettling, it simply does not matter whether the young man felt love or lust, whether he then merely forgot her or instead continued to love her after the narrative ends, and what if anything he might have chosen to do about it.

On occasion, however, our understanding of the typical fabliau "equilibrium" must encompass not only the return to a static position, but also the maintenance of a situation that, for example, permits a woman to continue seeing her lover, as apparent reward for having successfully deceived her husband once. In other words, when restoring the equilibrium of the situation, the authors of fabliaux may choose to present characters who resolve a temporary crisis in a manner that has permanent consequences. In *La Borgoise d'Orliens*, the husband, the beaten and happy cuckold, "Onques puis . . . / De nule rien ne la mescrut!" ("never again doubted her about anything," 321-22), and his enduring reassurance, we may assume, will permit his wife henceforth to see her lover at will. A number of fabliaux offer similar conclusions, with the husband reassured of an unfaithful wife's fidelity.[4]

Berengier au lonc cul goes considerably farther than these, however. This is the story of a woman who humiliates her cowardly husband, then spites him by inviting her lover to her home. When her

---

[3] Eventually, however, she not only surrenders to the inevitable but enjoys it (see 405-08), demonstrating once again the fabliau notion that all women want sex, even those who protest—or *believe*—that they do not.

[4] See, for example, *Les Braies au cordelier* and *Le Chevalier qui fist sa fame confesse*.

husband reacts in anger, she cleverly reminds him of his defeat and thus finds herself free to carry on her affair openly, presumably for as long as she wishes. A good many other texts offer similar conclusions. Interestingly, when the husband is victorious in the fabliau battle of the sexes, the only implication of the ending is that the wife will remain eternally submissive; when the wife wins—a less common occurrence, admittedly, but hardly rare—the conclusion either implies or explicitly states that she can continue to indulge her appetites. The latter fabliaux resolve crisis in favor of additional activity, from which the narrative potential for further disruption has been removed. In these texts, there *is* something implicit in the endings, and if we are justified in supposing that a wife may pursue her affairs, we must conclude as well that she can do so without fear of discovery. In other words, the end of such a text defines the limit of danger and drama, but not necessarily the end of action.

*

The discussion of endings also brings us to the end of discussions, and to the end of this volume. I have of course left much unsaid; in particular, and because they are better known,[5] I have dealt in cursory fashion with the "moralizing" fabliaux, discussing only one (*Le Vilain qui conquist paradis par plait*) in any detail. And I have surely left virtually untouched entire problems of fabliau criticism. However, my intent has by no means been to have the last word on the fabliaux; I have wanted instead to offer close readings of some individual texts and thereby, perhaps, to set the stage for other studies. I have wished to point out the diversity of the genre, the way some texts resist the attempt to generalize about *the* fabliaux.

Unfortunately, the very fact of organizing discussions around themes or problems leads us inevitably to emphasize, even if reluctantly, a commonality of themes, structures, attitudes, and comic devices. Even the preceding paragraphs of this conclusion have implied similarities—in terms of narrative overdetermination, the

---

[5] In some past anthologies and studies, the range of fabliaux represented extended from moral tales like *La Housse partie* to "inoffensive" anecdotes like *Estula* or, at most, the *Lai d'Aristote*. The linguistic and sexual frankness of many other fabliaux made them unacceptable for consumption by general audiences.

complexity of intrigues, the selectivity of narrators who leave unresolved problems, and the attitudes toward women—between two works, *Les Perdrix* and *Auberee*, that in other ways could hardly be less alike.

In fact, it will be helpful to acknowledge two apparently contradictory facts about the fabliaux. On the one hand, we can *understand* them only by acknowledging their traditional nature, their tendency to recycle materials and methods, and their resemblances to one another. On the other hand, we can *appreciate* them only if we respect them as discrete works of art and, especially, if we take the time to read them without preconceptions and to analyze them with some care.

Although all fabliaux deserve our attention, not all of them merit our respect, except as a matter of principle. More than a few are silly or pointless or vicious. More seriously, some are just inept narratives or failed attempts at humor. But we must give even those consideration if we are to understand the genre, or the broader range of narrative forms, to which they belong. And more to the point, the act of reading fabliaux will yield, as often as not, a heightened appreciation of some remarkable texts that may be masterpieces of either narrative economy or planned narrative disruption, of either clever rejoinders or physical punishments, of either subtle wit or bawdy humor, or sometimes comic absurdity. And we can best evaluate the achievements of fabliaux, whether excellent or execrable, by beginning not from generalizations about their character, their method, their humor, but from the individual text. Prerequisite to understanding the genre, in other words, is apprehending the text. My point of departure in this volume is thus my conclusion as well: our essential and most profitable activity is simply . . . reading fabliaux.

Works Cited

Editions and Translations

Chaucer, Geoffrey. *The Miller's Tale*, ed. Thomas W. Ross. A Variorum Edition of the Works of Geoffrey Chaucer, vol. 2, pt. 3. Norman: University of Oklahoma Press, 1983.

Dante Alighieri. *La divina commedia*. Florence: "La Nuova Italia," 1963.

Eichmann, Raymond, and John DuVal, ed. and trans. *The French Fabliau: B.N. MS. 837*. 2 vols. New York: Garland, 1984-85.

Guillaume de Lorris and Jean de Meun. *Le Roman de la Rose*, ed. Félix Lecoy. Paris: Champion, 1965-70.

Hellman, Robert, and Richard O'Gorman, trans. *Fabliaux: Ribald Tales from the Old French*. New York: Crowell, 1965.

Jodogne, Omer, ed. *Audigier et la chanson de geste, avec une nouvelle édition du poème. Le Moyen Age*, 66 (1960), 495-526.

Livingston, Charles H. *Le Jongleur Gautier le Leu: étude sur les fabliaux*. Cambridge: Harvard University Press, 1951 [with editions of Gautier's fabliaux].

Marie de France. *Lais*, ed. Alfred Ewert. Oxford: Blackwell, 1969.

Montaiglon, Anatole de, and Gaston Raynaud. *Le Recueil général et complet des fabliaux des XIIIe et XIVe siècles*. 6 vols. Paris, 1872-90.

Mort le roi Artu, ed. Jean Frappier. Geneva: Droz, 1964.

Noomen, Willem, and Nico van den Boogaard, eds. *Nouveau Recueil complet des fabliaux*. Vols. I-VI (VII-X in progress). Assen: Van Gorcum, 1983-.

O'Gorman, Richard, ed. *Les Braies au Cordelier*. Birmingham: Summa, 1983.

Studies

Avni, Ora. *The Resistance of Reference*. Baltimore: Johns Hopkins University Press, 1990.

Bédier, Joseph. *Les Fabliaux: Etudes de littérature populaire et d'histoire littéraire du moyen âge*. Paris, 1894; 6th ed., Paris: Champion, 1964.

Beyer, Jürgen. "The Morality of the Amoral." In *The Humor of the Fabliaux: A Collection of Critical Essays*, ed. Thomas D. Cooke and Benjamin L. Honeycutt. Columbia: University of Missouri Press, 1974, pp. 15-42.

Bloch, R. Howard. *Medieval Misogyny and the Invention of Western Romantic Love*. Chicago: University of Chicago Press, 1991.

——. *The Scandal of the Fabliaux*. Chicago: University of Chicago Press, 1986.

Burns, E. Jane. *Arthurian Fictions: Rereading the Vulgate Cycle*. Columbus: Ohio State University Press, 1985.

——. *Bodytalk: When Women Speak in Old French Literature*. Philadelphia: University of Pennsylvania Press, 1993.

Busby, Keith. "Courtly Literature and the Fabliaux: Some Instances of Parody." *Zeitschrift für romanische Philologie*, 102.1-2 (1986), 67-87.

Cooke, Thomas D. *The Old French and Chaucerian Fabliaux: A Study of Their Comic Climax*. Columbia: University of Missouri Press, 1978.

———. "Pornography and the Comic Spirit." In *The Humor of the Fabliaux: A Collection of Critical Essays*, ed. Thomas D. Cooke and Benjamin L. Honeycutt. Columbia: University of Missouri Press, 1974, pp. 137-62.

Coughlin, Ellen K. "Discontent with Deconstruction and Other Critical Conditions." *The Chronicle of Higher Education*, 17 February 1982, p. 21.

Davis, Judith. "*Audigier* and the Poetics of Scatology." In *Poetics of Love in the Middle Ages*, ed. Moshe Lazar and Norris J. Lacy. Fairfax: George Mason University Press, 1989, pp. 237-48.

Dubuis, Roger. *"Les Cent Nouvelles Nouvelles" et la tradition de la nouvelle en France au moyen âge*. Grenoble: Presses Universitaires de Grenoble, 1973.

Eichmann, Raymond. "The Antifeminism of the Fabliaux." In *Authors and Philosophers*. Columbia: University of South Carolina Press, 1979.

Genette, Gérard. *Figures III*. Paris: Seuil, 1972.

Gravdal, Kathryn. *Vilain and Courtois: Transgressive Parody in French Literature of the Twelfth and Thirteenth Centuries*. Lincoln: University of Nebraska Press, 1989.

Hart, Walter Morris. "The Fabliau and Popular Literature." *PMLA*, 23 (1908), 329-74.

Helsinger, Howard. "Pearls in the Swill: Comic Allegory in the French Fabliaux." In *The Humor of the Fabliaux: A Collection of Critical Essays*, ed. Thomas D. Cooke and Benjamin L. Honeycutt. Columbia: University of Missouri Press, 1974, pp. 93-105.

Honeycutt, Benjamin L. "The Knight and His World as Instruments of Humor in the Fabliaux." In *The Humor of the Fabliaux: A Collection of Critical Essays*, ed. Thomas D. Cooke and Benjamin L. Honeycutt. Columbia: University of Missouri Press, 1974, pp. 75-92.

Jodogne, Omer. "Le Fabliau." In *Le Fabliau et le lai narratif*. Turnhout: Brepols, 1975.

Johnson, Lesley. "Women on Top: Antifeminism in the Fabliaux?" *Modern Language Review*, 78.2 (1983), 298-307.

Koelb, Clayton. "Some Problems of Literary Taxonomy." *Canadian Review of Comparative Literature*, 4.3 (1977), 233-44.

Kotin, Armine Avakian. *The Narrative Imagination: Comic Tales by Philippe de Vigneulles*. Lexington: University of Kentucky Press, 1977.

Lacy, Norris J. "The Fabliaux and Comic Logic." *L'Esprit Créateur*, 16.1 (1976), 39-45.

——. "Fabliaux and the Question of Genre." *Reading Medieval Studies*, 13 (1987), 25-34.

——. Review of Thomas D. Cooke, *The Old French and Chaucerian Fabliaux. Res Publica Litterarum*, 2 (1979), 368-69.

——. "Types of Esthetic Distance in the Fabliaux." In *The Humor of the Fabliaux: A Collection of Critical Essays*, ed. Thomas D. Cooke and Benjamin L. Honeycutt. Columbia: University of Missouri Press, 1974, pp. 107-17.

Lanser, Susan Sniader. *The Narrative Act: Point of View in Prose Fiction*. Princeton: Princeton University Press, 1981.

Lorcin, Marie-Thérèse. *Façons de sentir et de penser: les fabliaux français*. Paris: Champion, 1979.

Ménard, Philippe. *Les Fabliaux: contes à rire du moyen âge*. Paris: PUF, 1983.

Minnis, A.J. *Medieval Theory of Authorship*. Missoula: Scolar, 1984; 2nd ed., Philadelphia: Univeristy of Pennsylvania Press, 1988.

Muscatine, Charles. *The Old French Fabliaux*. New Haven: Yale University Press, 1986.

Noomen, Willem. "Qu'est-ce qu'un fabliau?" *Atti* of the XIV congresso internazionale di linguistica e filologia romanza. Naples, 1981.

Nykrog, Per. *Les Fabliaux*. Copenhagen: Munksgaard, 1957; new ed., Geneva; Droz, 1973.

Pearcy, Roy J. "Investigations into the Principles of Fabliau Structure." In *Versions of Medieval Comedy*, ed. Paul G. Ruggiers. Norman: University of Oklahoma Press, 1977, pp. 67-100.

———. "Modes of Signification and the Humor of Obscene Diction in the Fabliaux." In *The Humor of the Fabliaux: A Collection of Critical Essays*, ed. Thomas D. Cooke and Benjamin L. Honeycutt. Columbia: University of Missouri Press, 1974, pp. 163-96.

Regalado, Nancy Freeman. *Poetic Patterns in Rutebeuf: A Study*. New Haven: Yale University Press, 1970.

Rychner, Jean. *Contribution à l'étude des fabliaux: variantes, remaniements, dégradations*. 2 vols. Neuchâtel, 1960.

———. "Les Fabliaux: genre, styles, publics." *La Littérature narrative d'imagination*. Colloque de Strasbourg, 23-25 avril 1959. Paris: PUF, 1961.

Schäffer, Hermann. *Über die Pariser Hss. 1451 und 22555 der Huon de Bordeaux-Sage: Beziehung der Hs. 1451 zur "Chanson de*

Croissant"; die "Chanson de Huon et Callisse"; die "Chanson de Huon, roi de Féerie." Marburg: Elwert, 1892.

Schaeffer, Neil. *The Art of Laughter.* New York: Columbia University Press, 1981.

Schenck, Mary Jane Stearns. *The Fabliaux: Tales of Wit and Deception.* Amsterdam: John Benjamins, 1987.

Tiemann, H. *Die Entstehung der mittelalterlichen Novell in Frankreich.* Hamburg, 1961.

White, Sarah Melhado. "Sexual Language and Human Conflict in the Old French Fabliaux." *Comparative Studies in Society and History,* 24.1 (1982), 185-210.

Zumthor, Paul. "La Brièveté comme forme." *Genèse, codification et rayonnement d'un genre médiéval: la Nouvelle,* ed. Michaelangelo Picone, Giuseppe De Stefano, and Pamela D. Stewart. Montreal: Plato Academic Press, 1983, pp. 3-8.

——. *Essai de poétique médiévale.* Paris: Seuil, 1972.

Index of Fabliaux

The following list includes all the fabliaux discussed in this volume. They are given in alphabetical order without the definite article (*le, la*) or the preposition *de*, which has simply been dropped when it begins a title. Following the title is the location of the text in the editions used; those editions are indicated by the sigla N (for Noomen and van den Boogaard), MR (Montaiglon-Raynaud), and, in one instance each, L (Livingston) and ED (Eichmann and DuVal). Full titles and publication information are given in the bibliography.

The italicized numbers following the reference to the edition indicate the pages on which that text is discussed or mentioned.

Brunain la vache au prestre, N, V, 39-48; *44-45, 92, 119, 124-25, 126, 127, 151.*

Cele qui fu foutue et desfoutue, N, IV, 151-87; *85.*

Cele qui se fist foutre sur la fosse de son mari, N, III, 375-403; *1-16, 17, 18, 19, 27, 48, 56, 58, 59, 72-73, 100, 110, 119, 128-29, 136, 154.*

Celui qui bota la pierre, N, VI, 125-44; *84, 125.*

Chevalier a la robe vermeille, N, II, 241-308; *92, 146.*

Chevalier qui fist parler les cons, N, III, 45-173; *100, 132.*

Chevalier qui fist sa fame confesse, N, IV, 226-43; *37, 41, 42, 59, 135, 156.*

Chevalier qui recovra l'amor de sa dame, MR, VI, 138-46; *31, 46-55, 86, 133.*

Chevaliers, des deus clercs, et les villains, ED, II, 192-95; *35.*

Chivaler et de sa dame et de un clerk, MR, II, 215-34; *76.*

Con qui fu fait a la besche, N, IV, 13-21; *90.*

Contregengle, MR, II, 257-63 (actually a variant version—MS. *B*—of the second half of *Deux Bordeors ribauz*, but the divergence is so strong that MR published it as a separate fabliau); *111.*

Crote, N, VI, 25-32; *16, 74, 123.*

Couille noire, N, V, 163-89; *2, 42.*

Couvoiteus et l'envieus, N, VI, 273-87; *138, 148.*

Dame escolliee, MR, VI, 95-116; *2, 41, 60-68, 72, 74, 75, 108-10, 126-27, 136, 141, 142, 151.*